Houdin and his son Émile performing their Second Sight act in the Robert-Houdin Theater in Paris.

From an illustration in the original French edition of Robert-Houdin's Memoirs.

The Magic Man

Jean Eugène Robert-Houdin surrounded by his automata and magic apparatus.

THE MAGIC MAN

The Life of Robert-Houdin

by
I. G. EDMONDS

THOMAS NELSON INC.

Nashville / New York

Also by I. G. Edmonds

Bounty's Boy
Hot Rodding for Beginners
Joel of the Hanging Gardens
The Khmers of Cambodia:
  The Story of a Mysterious People
Our Heroes' Heroes
Revolts and Revolutions
Trickster Tales

Second printing, February 1973

Text copyright © 1972 by I. G. Edmonds

Illustrations copyright © 1972 by Thomas Nelson Inc.

All rights reserved under International and Pan-American Conventions. Published in Nashville, Tennessee, by Thomas Nelson Inc. and simultaneously in Don Mills, Ontario, by Thomas Nelson & Sons (Canada) Limited.

Library of Congress Catalog Card Number: 71–181679
International Standard Book Number: O–8407–6146–5
Manufactured in the United States of America

To Annette

who likes to do magic tricks herself

Contents

Foreword

Do you remember the story of the lost horseshoe nail? It caused a horse to stumble. Its rider was thrown to the ground. The loss of the soldier caused the charge to fail. The entire battle was lost because of one little horseshoe nail.

Perhaps this incident never happened, but it is told and re-told to teach the importance of little things which can grow into something big.

This story of Robert-Houdin—"the father of modern magic"—is also a tale of some little things which were responsible for something very important. Jean Eugène Robert-Houdin's life was changed by a small mistake that seemed as trivial at the time as the lost horseshoe nail of the fable. But this mistake changed Jean Eugène's entire life. It turned a young watchmaker into a magician.

A magician, for all his fame, is an unimportant person compared to famous generals who win wars and change history. This bothered Houdin as he grew older. Sometimes he wished that he had remained a watchmaker. He felt that as a watchmaker he would have been more useful to his country than he was by making little tricks to amuse the people.

Then one day, the Arabs and Moors of Algeria began to revolt against France. An officer of the French Foreign Legion came across the Mediterranean Sea to visit the famous magician.

This man asked Houdin to wave his wand and make a war disappear!

The magician, who had amazed so many people with his tricks, was now amazed himself. But he did go to Algeria for his country. It is one of the strangest war stories ever told, but the truth is that Houdin did prevent a war with his magic.

To do it, he used things as trivial as the lost horseshoe nail. He used a tallow candle, the blade of a knife, some soot from a tiny flame, an old pistol, and a lot of personal courage.

In his lifetime Robert-Houdin performed many amazing tricks, but they are no less amazing than the wonderful life this unusual man led.

This is his story.

The Magic Man

1. A Call to Arms

Jean Eugène Robert-Houdin was a little sick from the tossing of the ship as it crossed the Mediterranean from France to Algeria, but he was even more sick of the jokes his fellow passengers made about his upset stomach.

He walked to the ship's rail as they moved into the harbor and looked at the domes and minarets towering above the twisting streets of the ancient city.

"It is just like the *Arabian Nights*," he said to his wife when she joined him on deck.

"It looks so strange," she said, her face clouding with worry. "Oh, I do hope Colonel de Neveu is here to meet us. I'm sure we will get lost in those crooked streets."

"Please, madame," Houdin said. "Never worry until there is something to worry about. There is our good friend, *le bon colonel*, on the dock. He has some soldiers with him."

He pointed across the water to where a tall French officer stood with a squad of Foreign Legionnaires.

"Who is that distinguished man with him?" Mme. Houdin asked.

"Oh, somebody," Houdin replied without interest.

He was too busy enjoying the strange sights to care about another Frenchman.

"Look!" he said excitedly. "There is a marketplace just beyond the docks."

He pointed to where colored awnings stretched over hundreds of little stalls. Men and women of a dozen nations made a colorful picture in their native costumes as they shopped.

A donkey loaded with ripe figs suddenly sat down in the middle of the crooked street. Its owner screamed and beat it with a stick. Houdin laughed with the shoppers when the little beast refused to move until bribed by a handful of figs from its load.

"Monsieur Houdin."

Jean Eugène turned to see the ship's captain hurrying across the deck toward him.

"Monsieur! Why did you not tell me you were so important a person? That is his Excellency the Governor of Algeria down there to meet you!"

"I did not tell you I was so important because I did not know it myself," Houdin said with a smile.

"Please come, Monsieur Houdin," the captain said. "The sailors are lowering the gangplank. You will be the first one off."

The French Foreign Legionnaires in their blue-and-white uniforms lined up as a guard of honor as M. and Madame Houdin left the ship. Colonel de Neveu and the governor greeted them warmly.

Then, as they turned to enter the governor's carriage, an Arab jumped on top of a barrel. He was tall and wore a curved sword stuck under the camel's-hair rope that belted his burnoose. His eyes flashed and his heavy black beard shook as he pointed to Houdin and shouted to the crowd.

"Doesn't he like me?" Houdin asked, stopping to watch the Arab with interest.

"The man is telling the crowd to open their eyes with wonder," the governor said with a smile. "Can you translate his exact words, Colonel?"

"But of course, Excellency," de Neveu said. "He is saying: 'Behold, O true believers! By the grace of Allah your unworthy eyes are looking upon the great marabout from France!'"

"Marabout?" Houdin repeated. "Is that something good or bad?"

"The Arabic word is *murābit*," de Heveu said. "We French have trouble saying it. We say marabout. It is the native name for a holy man."

"That does not mean the type of priest one sees standing on top of the minarets calling the faithful to prayer," the governor added. "The marabout is a wandering prophet who is supposed to be able to do miracles. He is making a lot of trouble for us."

Colonel de Neveu laughed as Houdin said, "Oh! Trouble-maker, eh? That's why he calls me a French marabout!"

"Hardly," the governor said. "These marabouts are doing a lot of tricks to convince the people that they have supernatural powers. They are the ones trying to start a revolt against France in Algeria."

"We hope you can destroy their power by exposing their tricks and by doing even greater tricks than they do," de Neveu said.

"I can only try," Houdin said. "Naturally, I would like to see some of this marabout magic before I start my own."

The governor shook his head, causing his drooping white moustache to shake so much Houdin thought it might drop off.

"Impossible," he said quickly.

"Unfortunately," the colonel said, "your show is scheduled for five o'clock. We have invited many important chiefs whose people are listening to these false prophets. And we have sent out many street shouters like this one to tell the people about your great magic."

"I know there is very little time," Houdin said, "but how can I do better tricks when I don't know what their tricks are?"

"That is true, your Excellency," de Neveu said to the governor.

The governor looked unhappy. It was time for his dinner, and he had little confidence that a magician could help them prevent a war.

"I see one of the rascals now," de Neveu said. "He is sitting in the marketplace. Perhaps we can watch him for a few minutes. You have less than two hours before your show opens, Monsieur Houdin. Can you make your preparations in so short a time?"

"I should have more time," the magician said. "But I must see a marabout's magic if I am to help you."

"I don't know," the governor said, still thinking of his dinner. "These people hate the French. Someone may try to kill you."

"That is not important," Houdin said quickly. "You asked me to come here and do a job. I cannot do it unless I know what I face."

"Very well," the governor said unhappily.

The colonel gave orders to his sergeant major to scatter the legionnaires through the crowd to make sure a fanatic would not try to kill Houdin and the governor.

Then the group crossed the street to watch the native magician. He was a tall Arab dressed in a white burnoose. In his right hand he held a large basket. In his left was a sharp thin sword. He shouted shrilly. His eyes were bloodshot and wild. His pointed beard made him look devilish.

"What is he saying?" Houdin asked the colonel.

"He says, 'When the true believers rise against the French

who oppress us, my magic will protect you from the swords of the Christian dogs the same way it protects this lad from my own knife,' " de Neveu translated.

The marabout put the basket on the ground. A skinny Arab boy came forward who wore only a soiled rag about his middle and looked half starved. He climbed into the basket and pulled the wicker lid shut on top of him.

"There is no God but Allah! Mohammed is his prophet!" the Marabout cried. "Thus shall the true believers be safe from the knives of the French dogs!"

He suddenly jabbed his sword into the basket. Inside, the boy screamed. The native magician yelled even louder, drowning the boy's cries.

He jabbed the sword again and again into the basket, from every possible angle. It seemed impossible that the lad inside could escape death.

Finally the prophet stepped back, breathing hard. As he did so, the lid flew off the basket and the boy jumped out unharmed.

"*Wah hyat Ullah*," the startled crowd cried. "As Allah liveth."

Many threw themselves on the ground and covered their heads. Others rushed forward reverently to touch the burnoose of the miracle man.

"You see what we are up against," de Neveu said to Houdin. "These people really believe this faker can perform miracles. They are ready to follow him and his kind in a revolt against France."

"I just don't see how that boy escaped being stuck," the governor said. "That villain stuck that sword in everywhere! Can you do a better trick than that, Monsieur Houdin?"

He sounded as if he didn't think so.

"It is a simple trick," Houdin said. "I think it came first from India. You notice the boy is half starved. He twists his body around inside the basket so the sword passes by his side. Then he quickly shifts to the other side so the magician can stab where he was before."

"Is that all there is to it?" the governor asked.

"Do not be so disappointed, Excellency," Houdin said. "You noticed how quickly the magician jabbed the sword in the basket. The boy did not have a second to waste. Both he and the marabout had to practice many hours to do this so well. It is a very dangerous trick. If either he or the boy had missed his timing, the lad would have been killed. Remember, the magician cannot see where the boy is."

"Can you do the thing also and show him up as a faker?" the governor asked.

"I have only Mme. Houdin for my assistant," the French magician said. "I'm afraid I have fed her too well. She would hardly fit in a small basket."

The governor and the colonel laughed. The marabout whirled around. He thought they were laughing at him. His swarthy face blackened with rage. He managed to smile with his mouth, although his eyes spat hatred at the Frenchmen. He bowed to Houdin and spoke rapidly in Arabic.

"He does not know that I understand his language," de Neveu whispered to Houdin. "He is smiling and acting friendly, but actually he is insulting us. Notice the natives. They are having a hard time keeping from laughing."

"We must pay him back in his own coin," Houdin said. His sharp eyes searched the Arab's costume for some object that would be useful in a plan he had in mind.

"He is saying, 'The short one is he whom the street shouters call the French marabout. He is no magician. He is a pig and the son of a pig who was himself the son of another pig! Watch, O true believers! Shortly I will do a miracle and dare this French pig to do the same.' "

The people in the crowd struggled to hide their mirth.

Women giggled behind their veils and a little boy rolled in the dirt.

"Let's leave here," the red-faced governor said. "It is not good for French dignity to stand here while this rascal makes a fool of us."

"Wait," Houdin said. "I must see this trick he challenges me to do."

"*Hai! Hai!*" the prophet shouted. He swung his sword in an arc about him. The frightened crowd fell back. The magician cleared a path and ran to the nearest street seller's stall. The merchant sat on the ground, frying little cakes over a clay brazier of glowing charcoals.

He overturned the coals onto the ground. The merchant groaned. He lifted his hands toward heaven and cried to Allah to protect his property. Since the marabout was such a holy man, he could not cut him down with his dagger as he would any other man who dared to spill his fire.

"There is but one God and his name is Allah!" the prophet cried.

He shook off his pointed sandals and stepped onto the burning coals with his bare feet. He walked across them and did not seem to be burned by the fire.

Houdin's eyes narrowed. He knew this must be a trick of some kind, but he had never been able to do the oriental firewalk himself. For the first time he started to wonder if he really could match the Arabs trick for trick.

Then the marabout stepped back. He opened the thick sash that circled his waist. He removed an old flintlock pistol. Before he could close the sash, Houdin glimpsed a French pocket watch and a clasp knife.

The Frenchman smiled, feeling better at once.

The Arab poured a measure of powder into the old gun. Next he put in wadding and then rammed a lead slug down the barrel. When the gun was primed, he fired it at the ground. The crowd and the governor jumped at the loud explosion. Houdin smiled. He knew what was coming next, and welcomed it.

The marabout reloaded the gun. Then he handed it to an old Arab in the crowd.

"Shoot at me!" he cried.

"No, no, holy one!" the man cried. "If I shot a marabout, I will burn forever in the fires of the devil, Shaitan!"

"And I will bring down the fires of heaven to burn you right now if you do not do as I tell you. Fear not, old man! My true magic will keep the gun from firing. Thus will it be also when the French dogs aim their guns at the true believer!"

The old man took the gun. His hand trembled. He brought up the muzzle until it pointed at the false prophet's chest.

"Oh, Allah! Protect the true believer!" the marabout cried.

The old Arab pulled the trigger. The hammer fell, and the gun did not fire. The crowd watched silently. A misfire from a faulty cap was nothing unusual in these old guns.

The marabout took the gun and pointed it at the ground. He pulled the trigger. The explosion was deafening. The lead slug plowed into the ground.

The crowd shouted in superstitious awe at this proof that the gun was good and that it had only been the priest's magic that kept him from being killed when the old Arab pulled the trigger.

Smiling nastily, the marabout took the gun by the barrel and held the butt out to Houdin. In perfect French he asked the European magician if he could cast a spell on the gun in a similar manner.

"Yes," Houdin replied. "I can do a trick with a gun. I prefer not to stop the bullet in the barrel as you do. I let it fire at me and catch the bullet in my teeth."

"Impossible!" the marabout cried.

"Not at all," Houdin replied. "I shall do the trick in the theater tonight. Please come as my guest and see it done."

The Arab smiled craftily. "A theater is for tricks," he said in French and then repeated his words in Arabic so the crowd could understand.

"Real magic—such as I do—is performed under Allah's sky. Let me fire this bullet at you right here. If you can catch it in your teeth, I will kiss your feet and worship you as my master."

"I could do so," Houdin said, "but unfortunately your great chiefs are waiting for me in the theater. It would insult them for me to perform this great trick in a marketplace first. I must first show them. You understand, of course."

"I understand that you are a faker!" the marabout cried.

At the edge of the crowd a donkey brayed loudly. The marabout laughed.

"See!" he cried. "Our long-eared friend has given his own and my opinion of the false magic of this faker from France."

The crowd joined his laughter. The governor's fat face reddened. Even the colonel looked embarrassed. "Come, Monsieur Houdin," he said. "We had best leave."

"Wait!" Houdin said.

He took a handkerchief from his pocket. He made a fist of his left hand and spread the handkerchief over it. The marabout, suspecting some trick, looked closely at the handkerchief. The crowd grew silent as they watched this duel between magicians. Their eyes were also on the handkerchief.

When everyone's attention was diverted to the handkerchief, Houdin's right hand slipped unnoticed into the sash girdling the marabout's waist. It came away clenched as if holding something.

Then Houdin let the handkerchief fall. Before it touched the ground he grabbed it. He wadded the square of cloth into a ball. This ball he laid on the palm of his right hand. He slowly started to unwrap it. Inside was an old French watch.

The crowd was not impressed. This was not marabout magic but the kind of thing any street faker could do.

The governor whispered to the colonel, "Is this dolt supposed to be the greatest magician in Europe?"

"That is what they say," the Legion officer replied.

"Then why doesn't he do something besides children's tricks?"

Houdin heard the angry whisper. His lips tightened, but it was the only sign that he gave of how much it hurt him. He said nothing while the crowd and the marabout jeered at him. He kept his hand outstretched with the watch in it.

"I will show you how this trick is done so every street urchin can be as great a magician as this French faker!" the marabout said.

He reached in his girdle for his own watch. His face turned blank when he didn't find it. A sudden look of suspicion shot across his eyes. He peered closely at the watch Houdin held.

Suddenly he shouted, "Thief! Robber! This is my watch. You have stolen it!"

"A mistake," Houdin said with a smile. "I intended to have the governor's watch fly into my handkerchief. Please take my apologies along with your watch."

He handed it to the Arab. The man looked at it suspiciously.

"Where is the chain? I had a short gold chain."

"Oh?" Houdin said, a puzzled look on his face. "The chain. Now where did my magic put that chain?"

He looked around, his face twisted in deep thought. His eyes lighted on a wide-eyed little Berber girl who was selling peaches.

"Ah!" he said. "That is where the chain went!"

He took a peach from her basket and gave her a franc piece in return. It was several times what the fruit was worth.

Gravely, Houdin took a pocket knife from his coat and cut a circle around the peach.

"Voilà!" he cried as he twisted the halves apart. "And inside we find the—oops! I'm very sorry. There is no chain there. Only the stone. Now I was sure . . . Now where can that chain be?"

He sighed and placed the two halves of the peach together. He covered them with his handkerchief, and when he drew the handkerchief away, the fruit was whole again. He smiled as he handed it back to the surprised child.

A man reached over and took it from her hands. He grunted in surprise when he found no sign of a cut.

Houdin bowed to the enraged marabout. "Ten thousand pardons and still one pardon more," he said. "I am a clumsy magician. Please be patient. I will find your chain if I have to open every peach in Algiers. I—"

Suddenly the donkey brayed again. Houdin snapped his fingers.

"Now I know!" he cried in triumph.

He walked over to where the little gray animal stood under its load of pottery while its master, a young boy, watched the magicians duel.

Houdin's hand went to the donkey's mouth and seemed to lift a short gold chain from under the animal's tongue.

"Does he always eat gold?" Houdin asked the boy, and then turned to give the chain back to its angry owner.

He bowed deeply to the marabout and to the crowd as a magician does when he finishes his act. Then he turned to Colonel de Neveu.

"Come, sir, I must hurry to the theater. I must not keep the chiefs and the sheikhs waiting."

2. The Challenge

They drove to the theater in the governor's coach. His Excellency's manner had changed. He was in a jovial mood.

"Monsieur," he said, "I know magicians are reluctant to tell how their tricks are done, but I hope this does not apply to other people's tricks."

Houdin smiled. "You want to know how the marabout kept the gun from shooting him? It is too simple, your Excellency. As you know, the powder will not explode without air. So this particular model gun was made with an air vent in the side. If this is stopped up, the gun will not fire."

"So simple as that!" the governor said.

"Yes, the marabout fired the gun. Then, as he reloaded, he cleverly put a stopper in the vent. And when he took it back from the Arab, he removed the stopper and the gun fired."

"But why didn't we see him do that?"

"One of the great secrets of magic is the ability to divert your audience's attention so you can do something you need to do without them knowing it."

"Will you do this same trick?" de Neveu asked.

"No," Houdin said. "If I do, the marabout will know how I did it. It is not enough for me to fool ignorant crowds. If I am to be successful in destroying the power of these false prophets for you, I must amaze and fool them as well as the people."

"This is an excellent trick," the governor said. "How can you top it?"

"I shall load a gun. If he comes to the theater tonight, I shall ask him to fire it at me. It will fire, and I will catch the bullet in my teeth."

"That is impossible!" the governor cried.

"That is what the marabout told me too," Houdin said with a smile.

"I saw M. Houdin do this trick in Paris," Colonel de Neveu said. "I understand that it is very dangerous."

"I have begged him many times not to do the trick anymore," Mme. Houdin said. "Did you know, Excellency, that the unhappy man who taught it to my husband killed his own son while trying to do the trick?"

"My word!" the governor said. "Is this true, Monsieur Houdin?"

"I am sorry to say that it is," the little magician said sadly. "Torrini was the magician's name. He became a very good friend of mine after he saved my life. Torrini was doing the trick in Italy when something went wrong. His son was shot in the head. It was all a terrible mistake, but Torrini never got over it. Years later he would cry like a baby when he recalled the tragedy."

"And you still do the trick yourself?" the governor asked. "Aren't you afraid the same thing will happen to you?"

"It is possible," Houdin admitted. "That is why I insist on being the one in front of the gun. If there is an accident, I must be the one who suffers."

"It is too great a risk," the governor said with a positive shake of his head. "You should not do it."

"But I must top the marabout's act," Houdin said. "If it helps to prevent a war, then I gladly take the risk."

"Well, now . . ." the governor began.

"In agreeing to help us, your Excellency," de Neveu said, "M. Houdin has become a soldier—a magic soldier!"

"Something bothers me, gentlemen," Houdin said, a frown crossing his face. "This marabout talked about his people being oppressed by the French. Is this true?"

"Do you know anything about the history of Algeria?"

"I am embarrassed to admit it, your Excellency, but I do not."

"Algeria was the site of ancient Carthage. You must remember the great general Hannibal and how he crossed the Alps to battle Rome. After Carthage fell, the Romans came. They were followed by the Arabs and the Moors, who intermingled with the native Berbers. Then, in the sixteenth century, the Turks came and occupied the coast.

"This mixture of warlike peoples kept Spain from taking over the region, and they turned the coast into a pirate stronghold. For years they were the terror of the sea. Finally the angry Americans sent a fleet in 1804 to stop the pirates. But by 1830 the corsairs had become so bad again that our own French government stepped in. We took over Algeria to put down the pirates. Eight years ago there was a bloody revolution against us. Many Algerians and legionnaires were killed."

"And now these fake holy men are trying to stir up another revolution," Colonel de Neveu said. "If we throw them in jail, they will become martyrs. We think it better to prove them fakers and thus destroy the people's respect for them."

"And for a moment back there," the governor said with a smile, "I thought the job was too big for you, Monsieur Houdin. Now I am sure you will succeed."

The carriage stopped at the theater. Houdin, his wife, and the colonel stepped down. The governor went on to his palace in the Casbah, or fortress, but promised to be back for the show.

It was only an hour before show time. Houdin quickly checked the stage and went to his dressing room. De Neveu went along. He smiled when Houdin put some needles in his mouth and some figs in his pocket. Then the hawk-faced little magician took a pistol from his trunk of tricks. He inspected it carefully.

"It would be embarrassing if it did not shoot," he said to de Neveu.

"I would be even more embarrassed if it did shoot at me!" the colonel said.

"It is only a trick, monsieur," Houdin said with a smile. "It is not a lot different from the tricks I did in the marketplace."

"Until my dying day I'll wonder how you made that peach whole again after cutting it in half. As for the watch, I suspect that you are a very good pickpocket, Monsieur Houdin!"

"You are too smart, *mon bon colonel*," Houdin replied. "Yes, every magician must be a good pickpocket. As for the peach—well, it was done this way. Everyone's eyes were on the coin I gave the little girl. They did not see that when I chose a peach from her basket, I slipped a second one up my sleeve. Then, under cover of the masking handkerchief, I exchanged it for the one I cut in two. Simple, eh?"

"Simple, yes, but it fooled us all!"

"All mysteries are simple when they are explained," Houdin replied.

He took a goldfish bowl filled with water and fish. He put a waterproof cover tightly over the top so the liquid would not spill. Then he hung the bowl on a hook attached to his belt. His long cape covered it.

The stage manager came to say it was almost curtain time.

Houdin, accompanied by his wife and the colonel, walked to the wings. Mme. Houdin would be his assistant, and the colonel would come on stage with them to be the interpreter.

"Please don't do the bullet trick," Mme. Houdin whispered as they waited for the curtain to rise.

"I must, my dear," he said. And then the curtain went up.

There was no applause. The hostile audience stared at the magician from France. They saw a thin man with a narrow face, a hawk nose, and flashing eyes. He was dressed in formal clothes and wore a long black cape lined with scarlet silk.

Looking back at them over the lighted candle footlights, Houdin saw a sea of dark, bearded faces. The sheikhs, chieftains, cadis (town magistrates), and marabouts had chairs in front. In back of them native soldiers and townspeople—Arabs, Moors, and Berbers—stood behind ropes. The soldiers had been brought in by the governor's orders. The marabouts had been trying to get them to revolt against their French officers.

Houdin bowed, and Colonel de Neveu introduced him in Arabic. Nobody applauded. Houdin motioned to his wife. She came on stage carrying some loose needles and a spool of thread on a silver tray. Houdin offered them to the chiefs for inspection. They refused.

He realized then that he had made a mistake. The Arabs considered such things women's articles. He would have liked to stop the trick and substitute another, but he realized that it would look strange to stop now. Unhappily, he pretended to swallow the handful of needles while actually slipping them into a secret pocket in his sleeve. Then he did the same with the spool of thread.

After a show of swallowing hard, he reached in his mouth and grasped the package of needles he had hidden in his cheek. He pulled, and twenty-five needles, all threaded on a single string, came out.

In Europe the illusion that he swallowed loose needles and thread and then pulled them out of his mouth, all threaded, was a big hit.

Here it was a failure. The fierce desert men resented his showing them what they considered a woman's trick.

Houdin forced himself to smile despite his failure. He continued his act. One amazing trick after another was performed as he worked hard to impress the cold-faced men who stared so hatefully at him.

He waved a scarf in the air, and a bowl of swimming goldfish appeared out of nowhere. He had cleverly slipped it out from under his cape and secretly snapped off the waterproof cover under the scarf.

He made a cone of paper and placed it over a seed. A fig tree about three feet high was under the paper when he removed it. There was real fruit on the tree. Houdin pulled it off and tossed the figs to the audience. No one would touch them.

This was disappointing. In France the punch of the trick came when someone bit into the fruit and excitedly cried out that it was real.

Houdin looked up at the governor's box. The official's face was red, and he glared angrily down at the magician.

"I guess he thinks I am a failure again," Jean Eugène told himself. "Perhaps he is right. Magic and war do not mix."

Houdin took a deep breath. Some of his lost confidence came back to him. He turned around and waved his hand toward Mme. Houdin, who stood against the black velvet backdrop. He slowly unsnapped his scarlet-and-black cape as he walked toward her.

Suddenly he whirled it in front of her. The scarlet silk made a flashing circle for a second. When he dropped it to the floor, Mme. Houdin had vanished.

The effect was so startling the audience gasped. Several of the more superstitious chiefs jumped to their feet as if about to run from the theater.

Houdin smiled and felt relieved. He knew that this was one trick the marabouts could not duplicate in the marketplace.

He picked up the cloak. He whirled it again, and the vanished woman was back on the stage. She was holding a silver tray on which were a pitcher and twelve small glasses.

An uneasy murmur ran through the theater. Everyone in the audience had seen magicians make things disappear, but this was the first time anyone had seen a full-grown, live human being vanish and reappear right before his eyes.

Even the Europeans in the audience were startled. Usually disappearing acts were done with girls standing in special closets. The magician would close the door and the girl would slip out through a trapdoor at the back. But all Houdin did was to flip a cape in front of his wife. In that brief second she vanished from the stage. And just as quickly she came back.

Houdin saw a tall man standing in the aisle. It was the marabout with whom he had had his magic duel in the marketplace. The false prophet's mouth was open in surprise. This gave Houdin a warm glow. There is no audience a magician enjoys fooling as much as another magician.

Houdin motioned for Colonel de Neveu to come closer.

"Tell them I challenge any of their marabouts to make a living person vanish as I did."

"Good," the colonel replied in a low voice, since many in the audience understood French. "This is wonderful, Monsieur Houdin. Our scheme will work after all. These false prophets will be discredited when they can't do the same thing."

"I hope you are right. Somehow it seems that this is too easy," Houdin replied. "After the challenge I will do the Inexhaustible Bottle trick. I will show them the empty pitcher Mme. Houdin is holding. Then I will pour six kinds of wine from the empty—"

"No! No! Monsieur Houdin, not wine! Anything but wine," the colonel said in a frightened whisper. "You will destroy all the goodwill your last trick has brought you!"

"Why? Everyone—"

"In France, yes. But not in Algeria. The Koran forbids any true believer to touch wine."

"I didn't know," Houdin said.

"I should have told you, but I thought everyone knew that Arabs do not drink wine."

"No, the fault is mine," the little magician said. "I've always been so wrapped up in my work that I never gave a thought to the ways of the rest of the world. I should have studied this country before I came here. I will not do the trick tonight. Later, when I can change it, I will pour coffee from the empty pot."

He motioned for Mrs. Houdin to remove the glasses and pitcher from the stage.

Colonel de Neveu started translating Houdin's challenge to the marabout.

"O sons of the Desert," de Neveu said. "Surely the Garden of Allah has never before seen so great a magician as M. Houdin. But greater even than magic is the word of truth. Now, many false prophets have come out of the desert to fill your ears with lies about their own supernatural tricks.

"M. Houdin desires me to tell you there is no supernatural. It is all tricks and he will expose the tricksters. He has asked me to throw this challenge in their faces. He asks—"

"This man speaks with the tongue of a snake!"

The Arab who interrupted was the marabout from the marketplace. He leaped to his feet, screaming his words.

"O true believers!" he cried. "Listen not to the lies of the infidel. I make true magic. Look, O children of Allah! Look on this miracle and wonder!"

He jerked the pistol from his sash just as he had done earlier in the market. He shoved it into the hands of a sheikh sitting near him.

"Shoot!" he cried. "Shoot at my heart!"

The Arab chieftain stood up. Gravely he pointed the gun at the holy man.

He pulled the trigger. It snapped and nothing happened.

"I'll call the Legion guard and have him thrown out," de Neveu said angrily to Houdin.

"No, no," the little magician said. "This is good. I'll beat him at his own game."

"I don't think you should try that dangerous trick of catching a bullet in your teeth—"

"O true believers!" the marabout cried. "Think you that this is a womanly trick such as this faker from France insults your eyes with? No, this is real magic, for I stopped this bullet in the barrel with my power! Look you well at this gun which I commanded not to kill me! I now withdraw the command!"

He pointed the gun at the floor. He pulled the trigger. The explosion was cannon-loud in the theater.

The audience broke into loud shouts of praise for the magician. The marabout whirled triumphantly to face Houdin on the stage.

"You! You who claim all magic is trickery, can you trick this gun into not killing you? If you cannot, O dog of France, then slink away before the honest eyes of these sons of the desert!"

When de Neveu translated, Houdin said, "I will permit you to fire your own gun at my heart. But I will not stop the bullet in the barrel for I am a braver man than you. I shall catch the bullet in my teeth as it flies through the air to kill me!"

De Neveu translated for the audience. He knew that the marabout understood French. A gasp ran through the theater. After seeing Mme. Houdin disappear so strangely, they were ready to believe that the Frenchman could catch a fired bullet in his teeth.

The Arab sneered. "I accept your challenge," he said in perfect French.

He ran to the stage, almost tripping in his haste.

Houdin smiled at him. "You wish to help me with this trick?"

"No, I wish to kill you," the Arab said.

He spoke in French, but many in the audience understood. They quickly repeated the words in Arabic. Laughter and applause rippled through the theater.

"If you can, then I give you my permission," Houdin said. "But I warn you, it will be hard. My magic is much greater than yours."

"You are a trickster. I am a real magician!"

"May I see the gun?" Houdin asked.

The Arab handed it to him. The Frenchman made a big show of inspecting it. As he did, Houdin clumsily slipped a tiny plug into the air vent to prevent the gun from firing.

The marabout's sharp eyes had caught the action. His dark face did not change, but Houdin noted the happy gleam in the other man's eyes.

"Now may I see the lead bullet?" Houdin asked, handing the gun back to its owner.

The marabout fished it from his girdle.

"Now," Houdin said, "mark it so you will know it is the same one that I will catch in my teeth."

The Arab's hand trembled so badly he dropped the slug. He snatched it up and made an X in the lead with the point of his dagger. Houdin took it back.

"Now I will load it into the gun," he said.

He dropped the lead bullet into the barrel of the muzzle-loading gun. He held it gingerly by two fingers so everyone in the audience could see it go in. Then he handed the gun to the Arab, who seated the load with a ramrod.

Houdin walked across the stage to take his target position. De Neveu saw the marabout remove the plug Houdin had inserted in the air vent to prevent the gun from firing. He rushed across to tell Houdin.

"Monsieur!" he whispered. "The rascal removed the plug! The gun will really fire. He will kill you!"

"Of course the gun will fire," Houdin snapped.

"But this is murder!"

"But yes, *monsieur le colonel!* And I will be the one murdering you if you don't stop interfering! I want the gun to fire at me. I must have it fire! Can't you understand that!"

"But I am afraid—!"

"But I am not!"

He turned away from the agitated officer and motioned to the marabout.

"Come," he said grandly with a flourish of his scarlet-lined cape. "Kill me, sir!"

"Monsieur Houdin . . ." de Neveu pleaded.

"Please," Houdin said in a whisper. "Do not take offense at my angry words. It is but part of the show. The audience can see your concern for me. That is good, for it will convince them I am in grave danger!"

"Well, aren't you?"

"After the bullet fires you will know. If I die, I was in danger. If I live, I was not. It is so simple, no?"

"No! It is not simple! Good luck, Monsieur Houdin!"

He stepped back as the Arab aimed the gun at his rival magic maker.

Houdin took a handkerchief from his pocket and placed it over his heart to give a white target. "I do not want you to miss," he said.

"I never miss when an enemy of my people is in my gun-sights!"

He leveled the gun.

"*Crack!*"

The sound of the explosion rocked through the theater. Houdin staggered and fell!

De Neveu shouted hoarsely. The governor leaped to his feet. The Arabs screamed in delight. The theater was a bedlam of noise.

Then suddenly the shouting cut off as if by magic. Everyone stared as the man they thought dead got to his feet. He opened his lips and showed a bullet between his teeth. He did not touch it with his hands, but let the lead drop to the stage.

"See if it has your mark upon it," he said to the marabout.

Then to de Neveu he added, "Please tell the audience I am sorry I fell, but the force of the bullet was so great it knocked me off my feet."

The marabout picked up the bullet. His hands trembled. His stricken face told the tense, silent audience that it was indeed the bullet he had marked and rammed into the gun barrel.

As he stared in amazement at the bullet, Houdin suddenly waved his cloak. The marabout disappeared! The spectators stared in horror, for they could see only Houdin, Mme. Houdin, and the colonel on the stage. The Arab had vanished. Then Houdin flourished his cape again. The marabout reappeared!

Fifty soldiers in the back of the theater broke and ran away in fright. The sheikhs muttered uneasily but kept their seats.

"It is a trick!" the marabout cried, finally shaking off his bewilderment. "Anything is possible on a stage! I challenge this French dog to do his cheap trick under the sun of Allah, where flickering candlelight will not aid him! O children of the Desert! Listen to the words of a true believer and be not blinded by the tricks of a faker!"

Houdin tried to keep smiling, but it was hard. He feared that the wily marabout had put him in a spot where he could not save his honor.

The Arab had put his finger on the heart of the matter. It was true that Houdin could not possibly make people disappear and reappear in the open. And he was not sure he could perform the bullet-between-the-teeth trick either under the brilliant light of the sun.

But he knew it would ruin their plan if he refused the marabout's challenge. De Neveu realized the trouble Houdin was in. He tried to help.

"I am sure M. Houdin would be delighted to do his tricks for you in the marketplace," he said hurriedly. "But it is impossible. We are going to the village of the Djendel tomorrow."

"Splendid," the marabout said. "And I will be there too! And I will bring my gun. We will see if M. Houdin can palm the bullet with everyone watching him under the bright sun of Allah!"

"We will welcome you," Houdin said.

He bowed to the audience as the marabout left the stage and the curtain fell. There was no applause, but he was pleased by the puzzled buzzing of voices as the audience filed out of the theater.

Later, in Houdin's hotel, both the governor and de Neveu questioned him closely about attempting the bullet trick in the open air.

"Can you do it?" the governor asked.

"I don't know," Houdin said. "I must think very hard."

"I could issue an order forbidding any open-air magic shows," the governor said.

"Oh, no!" Houdin said quickly. "That would ruin everything. No, gentlemen, I must invent a way to do the bullet trick that will stand the light of day."

When his visitors had left, Mme. Houdin closed the door behind them.

"Now don't you start," he said. "I've had enough arguing."

"You cannot use the paper bullet in the sunlight. On the stage, with only candlelight, it looks real enough. So when you palm the real bullet and put the little paper shell in the barrel, everyone is convinced you loaded the gun with a real bullet."

"That is true," Houdin said. "I cannot use the paper bullet. I am not sure I can use the method of Torrini either, which is to use twin guns. He let one be loaded, then, by diverting attention cleverly, switched it for one loaded with powder but no slug."

"But he made a mistake once and got the guns mixed up."

Houdin nodded, "And killed his son. I am not afraid of getting the guns mixed up. I am afraid of the eyes of the marabout. Remember, he is a magician too. He knows this is a trick, and he will not let himself be fooled again. If he suspects I am hiding an extra gun under my coat, he will jerk up my jacket and expose me."

"Then you will not do the trick?"

"I must!"

"But how?"

"I don't know. I must find a way. I don't want to do the gun switch as Torrini did it. I want to use the marabout's own gun, and I suspect it is impossible to find another so much like it that he would be fooled."

"Then what are you going to do?"

"Do you remember when the famous American, Mr. P. T. Barnum, visited us in Paris?"

She smiled. "Yes. He said you were a mechanical genius!"

"Oh, you know how these Americans love to exaggerate things! But although Mr. Barnum was not completely right about me, he was not completely wrong, either! I shall invent a new way to do this old trick."

"How will you do that?"

"With some simple articles I hope you will get for me. I need a candle, a small knife, and a spoon."

"Such strange things to do a trick with."

"Oh I don't know," he said with a smile. "My whole life has been a magical trick. And some very strange things helped me perform it. Do you know what they were? Well, I will tell you. It happened to be a mouse, a hole in my shoe, a worthless book, a bird cage, a pain in my stomach, and a merchant's mistake. Yes, madame, these strange things combined to make me a magician."

"You are teasing me," she said.

"No, it is true. Now go to bed. I have work to do."

After she had left, Houdin walked to the window. He stood for a time looking at the brilliant stars speckling the sky over the ancient city of Algiers.

He smiled again as he remembered the strange things that made him become Houdin the Magician. And his thoughts drifted back to the long-ago days of his boyhood.

3. A Mouse and a Magic Book

Jean Eugène Robert was born on December 6, 1805. His father was Prosper Robert, a watchmaker of Blois, a town on the Loire River south of Paris.

His earliest memory of childhood was the wonderful workshop of Colonel Barnard. The old man had a shiny bald head, a stomach like Santa Claus, and a temper fitting the old soldier that he was. And for some reason Jean Eugène could never understand, the better the colonel liked someone, the louder he shouted at him.

The old man's workshop was a fairyland for a six-year-old boy. During Napoleon's invasion of Egypt, Colonel Barnard had been captured by the British Army. During the three years he spent in prison he had learned to make toys to pass away the lonesome hours. When he came back to Blois to live on his pension, he continued to make toys.

Jean Eugène would sit by the hour, his eyes wide, as the old man's twisted fingers turned out one treasure after another.

One day as the old man was filing a piece of metal into a tin soldier, he was called away for a few minutes. He laid the half-finished toy and the file on his workbench.

"Now you sit right there, young man," he said to Jean Eugène. "This is a real tough soldier and I fear he will run

away even though half finished. Keep an eye on him. If he
escapes, I'll have you shot at sunrise!"

"*Oui, monsieur*," Jean-Robert said. "Yes, sir. I'll guard him
with my life!"

When the colonel had gone, he sat looking at the roughly
shaped metal. It took a lot of imagination to see a soldier in
it. The legs and body were shaped, but the head and musket
were just blobs.

Without thinking, he picked up the file. Slowly he rubbed
it across the metal as he had seen the colonel do. He felt a
thrill. His heart beat faster as he saw tiny chips of metal roll
up. He pressed harder and soon forgot all else as he joyously
cut away at the head of the tin soldier.

He was so engrossed in his work that he did not hear the
old soldier come back. The first Jean Eugène knew he was
there was when he heard a roar.

"What is *this*, you young scamp!" the colonel cried.

"Oh!" Jean Eugène dropped the file. He tried to scramble
down from the high stool at the workbench. He caught his
leg and would have taken a bad fall if the colonel had not
caught him.

Instead of sitting him down, the old man raised Jean
Eugène up until their faces were level.

"I—I—I'm sorry, sir," Jean Eugène said miserably. "I didn't
mean to ruin your little soldier. I was just—"

"Just *what?*" the colonel roared.

"Just—just justing—I guess. Please, Colonel! Don't send me
away. Beat me, but don't make me go home. Let me stay and
watch you, and I promise never, never to touch anything
again."

"But I am taking you home," the colonel shouted, his voice
getting even louder. "And I shall tell your father what I
think."

"Please, Colonel, I promise—"

"Who taught you to file like this?"

"Nobody. I just watched you. I'm so sorry I ruined it."

"Who said you ruined it? Stop making excuses about something that never happened. This is marvelous work for a six-year-old."

He took off his leather apron. "Come," he said. "We will tell your father. He will be delighted too."

They hurried across the cobblestone street. A wooden sign swung in the wind. A picture of a clock and the words "Prosper Robert, Watchmaker" were painted on it.

"Monsieur Robert!" the colonel cried. His big voice made Jean Eugène's father jump.

"What mischief has the child done now?" he asked. "Just tell me and I will punish him later. I am too busy with these watches to stop now."

"No, no!" the colonel cried. "I want to tell you about his talent. While I was out of my shop he took my file. His cutting was beautiful! Why, it is just as if he had been born with a file in his hand. He will make a splendid craftsman."

Prosper Robert jumped to his feet, scattering the parts of a watch across the workbench.

"No son of mine will ever be a craftsman," he cried, his face red with anger.

"But Papa, I love to work with tools," Jean Eugène said. "I want to make beautiful things like you and the colonel do."

"Get such notions out of your head," Prosper Robert said crossly. "And Colonel, I will thank you to stop putting such ideas in the child's mind. I do not intend for him to be a craftsman. I want him to be a lawyer."

"A lawyer! But this is awful. Surely, Monsieur Robert, you are making the little joke, no?"

"Please, Papa, I want—"

"Quiet! Quiet, both of you. Stop looking as if you think I am some ogre. I have only the boy's good at heart."

"But if this is what the boy wants to be—"

"What does it matter what he wants to be now? Later he will thank me. Look at me, Colonel. I have spent my whole life working on watches. And if I do say so myself, I am a very good watchmaker."

"Yes, yes, of course, Monsieur Robert. You are a fine craftsman."

"*Oui,* a fine craftsman who has worked a lifetime, but has not saved enough money to bury himself if he died tomorrow. No, I will not have my son starving. He will be a lawyer."

"But you cannot do this! Look at the poor boy's face. See how badly it hurts him to hear you talk so."

"It is for his own good. And do not tell me what to do. He is my son!"

"Well, I have his company more than you do. He is in my shop more than he is in yours."

"Colonel, I know that you have the boy's good at heart, but please believe me, I know what is best for him."

No amount of arguing could change M. Robert's mind, but the colonel was not defeated. Later he told the unhappy boy, "Now don't you worry. I will keep talking to him. And my words will be just like a file. I will gradually wear him down."

But although Colonel Barnard was right about Jean Eugène being a born craftsman, he was wrong about filing down Prosper Robert's determination to make his son a lawyer.

For six years the two stubborn men argued about the future of the boy as Jean Eugène grew up. When the twelve-year-old got on a coach to go away to school, Prosper and the colonel were there to see him off. The last thing he heard as the coachmen whipped up the team was the colonel's bawling voice: "And I tell you as I've told you a thousand times, you cannot make a lawyer of a born mechanic!"

The school was in Orléans, up the Loire River. Jean Eugène quickly found that he had exchanged one father for another just like him. For the next six and a half years, Abbé Lariviere —that strict but kindly father—constantly told the growing boy that he must put away his tools and spend more time at his Latin if he hoped to make anything of himself.

Jean Eugène worked hard and was a good student, but he could not leave his beloved tools alone. They were his play. While the other children romped and chased each other about the grounds, Jean Eugène worked with his tools.

Naturally the others laughed and made fun of the boy for his strange ways. But this did not last long. Soon after his arrival at the school he became a hero to the other boys, and they were never again to poke fun at him.

The students had a science class. That day they were studying about pumps and how they had been used to lift water since the days of ancient Egypt. That evening, after his studies were done, Jean Eugène built a little pump that would actually pull water. To this he added a little machine to make it work. It was a treadmill, and a small mouse he had caught in a trap ran on it to make the pump move.

Unfortunately, it was only a very small mouse and the pump had many parts. The mouse could just barely cause it to move.

For once the other children were interested in something he had done.

"You need a rat instead of a mouse," one of the larger boys told him.

"I know," Jean Eugène said. "Do you know where I can get one?"

The older boy, whose name was François, winked at his companions. "I sure do," he said. "I will tell you if you are brave enough to go there."

"Oh, I'm brave enough," Jean Eugène said quickly.

The other boys had difficulty smothering their laughter.

"It is the *dungeon!*" François cried.

"Where is that?" Jean Eugène asked.

François looked disappointed. He expected to see fright on the other boy's face when he mentioned the terrible place.

"You don't know what the dungeon is?" he asked, surprised.

"He's only been here ten days. Nobody has been put in it for a month," one of the others said.

"Well, it's a dark room in the basement of the school. It is a very lonesome and scary place and there are big rats who live in holes in the walls. It is where the Abbé puts us when we break the school rules."

"Sure," one of the other boys said with a grin. "You can get a big mouse there—if you're not afraid!"

"I'm not afraid," Jean Eugène said stoutly.

"I'll bet you are too! I dare you to go in the dungeon!"

"Yeah! Yeah! We dare you!"

Jean Eugène looked solemnly at the jeering gang. Once in Blois he had had trouble because he took a dare rather than be thought a coward. After it was over and he had stopped smarting from the whipping his father had given him, the wise old colonel told him how to handle people who dared him.

He waited until everyone in the group of boys stopped shouting at him. Then he said, "I guess I would be afraid if I were alone, but I won't be with you along."

He looked at François when he spoke.

"Who—me?" The older boy stepped back. Then he said uneasily, "You're going to go alone!"

"Oh, no," Jean Eugène said. "Someone must go along, so they can see that I am not afraid in there. I want you."

"Go on, François," one of the others said.

"Well, you go if you're so brave!" the older boy snapped.

Soon they were all quarreling over who should go along and watch Jean Eugène. No one wanted to go. So when François said, "Ah, who cares about that old dungeon anyway," they were all ready to agree.

"Come on!" François said. "Let's play soldier. I'll be Napoleon!"

And they rushed off, leaving Jean Eugène looking sorrowfully after them. He didn't care because he was left out of their game. To him, running and jumping was silly when he could have so much fun making things with his tools. What he wanted was for them to like him. For a moment he had had their admiration with his little pump.

Sadly he opened the door of the treadmill and let the little mouse scamper out. He stood looking at the pump he had worked so hard to make. "I'm not afraid of the dark," he said at last. "I'll get me a bigger mouse!"

Supper was at sundown in the college. The good Abbé did not believe in wasting expensive candles. Besides, in his younger days he had known Benjamin Franklin in Paris and had once heard the famous American say, "Early to bed and early to rise, makes a man healthy, wealthy, and wise."

It was a saying his students became very sick of, for they heard it twice a day during the seven years they spent at the college. They heard it at night when the Abbé shooed them off to bed, and again in the morning when he woke them up, for at daybreak they hated to leave their beds as much as they had hated to get in them the night before.

As soon as they were sent to the dormitory, Jean Eugène grabbed his little trap and slipped down the stairs to the basement of the old building.

It was so dark he could not see. Suddenly he knew that he had been wrong. He *was* afraid of the dark! The wind was rising. The old house creaked and groaned. He clutched his little trap tighter and shivered.

But he never once thought of going back. All his life he was to be this way. He was more afraid of letting others *know* he was scared than he was of the things that frightened him in the first place. Some classmates had seen him go, so he couldn't return.

This was what made him feel his way through the basement darkness. It was also what made him face the most dangerous trick of his life forty years later in a little village in Algeria.

Finally he found the dungeon door. It was a basement room. There was a very small window near the ceiling. A little moonlight came through, so he could dimly see his way around.

He set the trap, baiting it with a piece of bread he had brought from the supper table. But he lost the bread and caught no mouse, for the spring on the door of his trap had broken, and the mouse escaped.

He refused to go back upstairs and let the other children know he had failed. He took off his heavy leather shoe and propped it up with the open end down, using little sticks broken from the trap. There were still a few crumbs left in his pocket. He put these under the shoe, and waited.

It seemed a long time before he saw a dark shadow move across the dust-covered floor. It slipped under the four pegs holding the upside-down shoe. Jean Eugène reached over quickly and knocked the shoe down on top of the surprised mouse.

The little rodent scrambled wildly inside the shoe. It climbed up the leather and into the toe as it frantically sought a way out of the footgear prison. Jean Eugène pressed the tops of his high shoe tightly together to keep the mouse from escaping and turned the shoe over.

Now that the suspense of trapping was over, he suddenly was aware of how fearful a place the dust-covered room was. His teeth chattered. He turned and fled up the stairs. By the time he got to the upper hall, his fears were gone. He was so tickled by his success that he burst into the dormitory crying, "I got one! I got one!"

The startled boys sat up in bed. François cried in a loud whisper, "Be quiet! You'll awake the Abbé!"

Jean Eugène put the shoe with the mouse in it sideways on the floor and set one leg of his cot on the closed shoetops to keep the little rodent from getting out.

He had no sooner done this than he heard the heavy clump of the schoolmaster's feet in the hall. There wasn't time to get undressed and into bed.

He was still standing there, trying to decide what to do when the Abbé Lariviere appeared at the door.

"What is this noise!" he cried. "I told you—"

He stopped when he saw Jean Eugène. "What are you doing up and dressed?" he asked.

Then he noticed how dirty the boy was. "Where have you been? Don't stand there, boy! Answer me at once!"

"I—I—" Jean Eugène stopped. He didn't want to tell the truth, but it was hard to lie to a man like the Abbé. "The dungeon, sir. I went to the dungeon."

"The dungeon? What is the dungeon?"

The Abbé's assistant, an old man named Marchal, had followed the schoolmaster into the room.

"Sir," he said, "that is what the students call the old room in the basement where we put those two boys two years ago when they were so bad we could do nothing with them."

"I remember," the Abbé said.

"The older students like to tease the newcomers by telling them you put everybody who misbehaves in there," Marchal said.

"Ha!" said the Abbé. "I see now. The boys have been teasing you, and you went down to show them you were not afraid."

"It was very brave," M. Marchal said. He was always standing up for the boys.

"Yes, but it was wrong. He must be punished. Perhaps I should lock him up in the dungeon!"

"The way he went down there alone I don't think that would frighten him."

"I suppose not," the Abbé said peevishly. "I suppose he would enjoy it. Well, I can't stand here wasting a good candle. Go to bed, young man. I'll think of some punishment in the morning."

While the Abbé was in the room, all the students had acted as if they were sound asleep. But after the two old men left, they all sat up in bed. The boy next to Jean Eugène said, "Are you lucky! When the Abbé gives punishment he does it right then. When he says he'll do it tomorrow, he never does."

The boy on the other side said, "Did you really go in the dungeon?"

"And was it scary?" another whispered.

"Sort of," Jean Eugène said happily as he crawled into bed.

He was soon asleep and dreamed that he had built a pump as big as a house. Ten thousand little mice ran around and around to give it power. It brought water from the well into the school, and the Abbé was very pleased.

When morning came, however, the glow vanished, and Jean Eugène found himself in trouble again.

"Early to bed and early to rise, makes a man healthy, wealthy, and wise!" The Abbé's booming voice rocked off the walls of the dormitory.

The boys tumbled out of bed. Jean Eugène was among the first up. He looked down at the shoe where the mouse was imprisoned. He blinked in surprise and then felt so sick he sat down on the side of the bed.

There was a hole in the side of his shoe where the mouse had gnawed its way to freedom while its captor slept.

"What will the Abbé say?" he whispered in a stricken voice.

As it happened, the good Abbé had plenty to say. He said it in a loud voice that boomed across the courtyard to the tune of a whistling switch.

It was a painful experience for Jean Eugène, but it made him a hero with the other boys. For the first time in his life he learned the joy of being applauded by a large group.

And at that moment he took the first unconscious step toward turning Jean Eugène Robert into Robert-Houdin, the great magician.

The second step came a little later. He had grown into a teen-ager and was on summer vacation in Blois. He was walking along the Loire River, dreading the trip back to Or-léans for his last session at the school.

Suddenly his thoughts were broken by the sound of a trumpet bellowing in the distance. It was such an odd sound that he walked toward it.

When he found the player, it turned out to be a very strange-looking man. He stood at the back of a cart pulled by a donkey. Jean Eugène looked at the maroon frock coat trimmed with silver frogs and was not impressed. He had started to turn away when the man put down his horn.

"Ah, one moment, my young man," he said. He had a deep, agreeable voice, and a friendly smile split his sunburned face. "I see you are leaving, but before you do, please leave my little friend."

"Your little what?" Jean Eugène asked. "I have nothing of yours."

"Oh, I am not blaming you, young sir," the tall man said. "I blame Lucifer. Please open your mouth."

"I will not open my mouth!" Jean Eugène retorted, nettled

by the man's manner. He forgot that he had to open his mouth to speak.

The gaudily dressed man's hand flashed toward Jean Eugène's open mouth. His hand was empty. This the boy would have sworn, but it came away from Jean Eugène's mouth with a tiny white mouse.

It scampered across the man's hand and up his arm. It paused on his shoulder and looked back at the openmouthed boy. A murmur of wonder rippled through the crowd that had gathered around the mountebank.

"Gentlemen," the magician said, sweeping the entire group with a commanding eye, "do not mistake me for one of those scurvy beggars who want to dredge a few centimes from your pockets. Pooh! Money means nothing to me. When I need it, I do like this!"

He pushed up the sleeves of his maroon coat, so that all could see he had nothing up them. Then he turned his hands over to prove that there was nothing there either.

This done, he reached into the air and plucked from nowhere a silver franc coin.

A trickle of applause went through the crowd. The man bowed gratefully and took a handkerchief from his pocket.

Jean Eugène still stood with his mouth open, staring in startled wonder at his first magic show.

"No, gentlemen," the mountebank said. "I am here only to help my fellowman. This I do by bringing a little pleasure into your lives with my little tricks.

"You behold in me the celebrated Dr. Carlosbach! I have a most enormous talent which I cannot tell you about due to my great modesty. But of course, that you will be able to see for yourself."

He flipped the handkerchief to show that it was empty and then folded it into a small square. When he undid the folds, another silver franc piece had miraculously found its way into the folded cloth.

Jean Eugène was lost in a world of wonder. Suddenly the Great Carlosbach became in his eyes the greatest man in the world.

"Oh," he said breathlessly as he watched trick follow trick, "I *wish* I could do that!"

After he had amused the crowd for some minutes, the Great Carlosbach put aside his tricks. He also forgot that he had no use for money and started selling his stock of wares to the assembled people.

Among the great treasures he was willing to part with —"for the benefit of my fellowman, for whom I have only the greatest love"—were some little booklets which Carlosbach assured his audience contained the secrets of every trick he had done that day.

The price was fifty centimes. Jean Eugène gulped. He had that much in his pocket, but it was to pay for his meals on the long coach ride to Orléans.

He hesitated only a moment. The thought of being another Carlosbach was more important than the three meals he would miss.

"I'll take one," he cried. "Will it really make me a magician?"

"It will tell you how I do my trick. That I guarantee," the Great Carlosbach said with a smile.

Clutching his treasure, Jean Eugène sat down on the curb and started reading. Swiftly his delight turned to puzzlement. He read the first page twice. There was a simple woodcut picture showing a hand taking a coin from the air. The explanation under it said only: "The coin is cleverly palmed where it cannot be seen by the audience and then flipped up between one's fingers as they reach into space."

"But what does he mean by 'palming'?" the bewildered boy asked himself.

He quickly went through the booklet. It was all the same. The instructions were too sketchy. His face reddened with anger at the way he had been cheated. He went over where Carlosbach was repacking his cart.

The magician looked up blandly at the angry boy.

"I want my money back," Jean Eugène said. "This book is no good!"

"You are obviously a lad who is seldom wrong," Carlosbach replied with a smile, "but this is one time that you are. It is an excellent book. I wrote it myself."

"I can't do any of the tricks in here. You promised me my money back. I want it."

"Well now, being as you are such a bright lad, you will recall that I said—and guaranteed—that this fine book will explain how *I* do my tricks. And so help me, it does that. You admit this, do you not, sir?"

"It tells how you do them, but it does not tell me how to do them."

"Oh, but I didn't guarantee *that*," the Great Carlosbach said with a smile. "After all, young man, if everyone could do these tricks, how would I eat?"

He climbed into his cart and drove off, leaving the angry boy standing in the cobblestone street.

4. Watchmaker or Magician?

It was many years before Jean Eugène realized that for all the loss of his fifty centimes, he had received many times the value of the fifty centimes from the Great Carlosbach.

For his money he got only a worthless book and a hungry stomach that grumbled all the way to Orléans. But in him had been kindled a love of magic and sleight-of-hand tricks that would make him world-famous as a magician.

But many years of trouble and work lay ahead of the boy before the world was to sing his praise.

As he was nearing the end of his school years, he spent most of his free time working on a gift for his father. For nearly seven years both Prosper Robert and the Abbé Lariviere had never lost an opportunity to tell him how much more he could profit from Latin and Greek than from his beloved tools. He listened dutifully but spent every spare moment at his work. He still wanted to be a craftsman, and the gift was to show his father how good he was at it.

It was then 1823, and mechanical toys, called automata, were very popular in France. These were elaborate gadgets operated by clockworks.

Jean Eugène made his in the form of a snuffbox. When the lid was raised a tiny hunter lifted his gun. At the same time, the clockwork wheels inside caused an even tinier rabbit to leap up. A lever struck a hidden gong that sounded like a gunshot and the rabbit fell dead. It was beautifully made and showed great talent, for the boy had filed every piece of it himself.

However, Prosper Robert was not pleased. He knew it was a silent plea from the boy to work in the watchmaking shop with his father.

Very angry at the stubborn way his son clung to the idea of becoming a watchmaker, Prosper Robert insisted on apprenticing Jean Eugène to the Maître Roger, a prominent lawyer in Blois.

It was to be an unhappy experience for everyone. Jean Eugène hated the tedious job of copying legal papers and running errands for the lawyer and his ill-natured chief clerk.

There was only one bright spot in the dingy office. This was a large cage of canaries that stood in one corner of the law office. One of Jean Eugène's jobs was to clean the birdcage. Before long he was making gadgets for the cage. He made a little trap which imprisoned one bird when he came to eat seeds from the feed cup. There he stayed until another bird came to eat. His pecking released the trap.

The hot-tempered chief clerk continually berated him for wasting time that should have gone to copying briefs for the law cases. Each time Jean Eugène promised to do better, but somehow he always forgot.

Then one day, after he had been a law clerk for a year, his master, Maître Roger, called him into the back office. The old lawyer pushed his glasses up on his forehead and looked at the young man much as he might look at a witness in court.

"Monsieur Robert," he began, speaking very formally, "when you came to work in our office you were aware that it was to devote yourself to business."

"*Oui, m'sieur,*" Jean Eugène said.

"It was not to satisfy your thirst for pleasure."

"*Oui, m'sieur.* Uh—I mean, no, sir. It was not."

The old lawyer sighed. "See," he said, "your mind is off on something else. You can scarcely hear me talking to you. I fancy you are really thinking of some new gadget to annoy my canary birds."

"Monsieur Roger, I am very sorry. I will do better. I promise you, sir."

"Let me see," Maître Roger said with a wan smile, "this must be the thirty-third, or is it the thirty-fourth, time you have made me such a promise. I greatly fear that this must be the last warning I give you. You paid no attention to the others. I suspect you will pay no attention to this one as well."

"I will try very hard, sir."

"For how long? Fifteen minutes? And then your mind will be off planning some mechanical gadget while your fingers, with no mind to guide them, make big ink blots on my legal papers."

"Sir—" the boy began.

The old man held up his hand. "Please. We waste our time. Whatever made you think you wanted to be a lawyer anyway?"

"Well, sir, I did not want to be one. I want most of all to be a magician, but I know that is impossible."

"I should hope so, for your own sake!"

"And since I can't do magic tricks, I would like most of all to be a watchmaker. I know my father says that watch-makers don't make enough money, but I do not wish to just repair clocks as he does. I want to go to Paris and build great automata run by clockworks and to make fine chronometers for ships at sea and—!"

"Yes, yes," the lawyer broke in. "I am busy and I must go to court. However, I understand how you feel. That is the work you should do."

That afternoon the lawyer again called Jean Eugène into his office.

"I spoke to your father. I told him that I had studied you for a year and felt convinced that you will never make a lawyer. But at the same time I was convinced that you would make an excellent craftsman."

"What did he say, sir?" the boy asked.

"Oh, he argued," the lawyer said with a smile, "but arguing is my own profession. He did not have a chance! So, Jean Engène, he has promised to apprentice you to your cousin, since he does not have the time to teach you himself. At long last you will become a watchmaker."

Jean Eugène's cousin Louis was a kindly man and wanted to help the lad. However, he was just a simple clockmaker and could teach him only so much.

There was, he told the boy, a very fine set of books on the more advanced aspects of watchmaking in a bookseller's shop across town.

That night when the shop had closed, Jean Eugène went to the bookseller's place. It was near closing time there too. Several people were in the shop and the single clerk was badly rushed. Since he did not have enough money for the entire set, Jean Eugène asked for only the first volume.

The clerk reached up on the top shelf and pulled down a large book. He shoved it across the counter and Jean Eugène paid him two francs. Both he and the clerk were in a hurry. The clerk wanted to shut up shop and Jean Eugène was eager to get home to dinner.

It was not until he had eaten and gone to his room that he discovered the mistake. Instead of Berthoud's *Watchmaking*, he had an old worn book called *Scientific Amusements*.

Looking at the Table of Contents, he saw listed such previously unheard-of things as "How to Cut Off a Pigeon's Head and Bring It Back Alive" and "How to Make an Orange Tree Grow from a Seed and Bear Fruit in One Minute."

Enthralled, he sat down at his desk. The candle burned lower as he read avidly about miracles he had never even dreamed were possible.

Since the country faker Carlosbach was the only magician he had ever seen, he was unaware that magic consisted of more than a few sleight-of-hand tricks. Now for the first time he got a glimpse of the fantastic tricks possible with the proper stage setting.

The candle burned lower, but he did not notice it until the flame went out. It was only then that he closed the book. He was too excited to sleep.

He went to the window. For a long time he stood there looking at the stars and dreaming of himself as a great magician doing his tricks before kings and queens.

In the morning, as soon as there was enough light to see the words, he got up. He could not waste even one precious moment. Clumsily he dressed himself while bending over the book, reading.

Forty years later he wrote in a book of his own, "I fear I shall be accused of exaggeration when I say that the discovery of this book caused me the greatest joy I had ever experienced. The resemblance between the two books and the hurry of a bookseller were the commonplace causes of the most important event in my life."

Thereafter Jean Eugène studied the magic book every time he got a chance. It was much better than Carlosbach's little booklet, but he realized that it could not make him a magician. It could show him the way, but he had to acquire the skill himself.

There then lived in Blois an old man who had once been a juggler. Jean Eugène felt that a juggler's quickness of hand would help him master the tricks described in his book.

He paid the juggler ten francs for lessons. In a few months he had learned all the old man could teach him. At the same time his skill had reached the point where he could do a few parlor magic tricks. The applause these brought only made him more eager to become a professional magician.

He learned that palming is one of the basic tools of the magician. He worked hard to master this ability to hold something in the palm of the hand while the fingers hang free and limber, giving the impression that there is nothing in the hand.

Jean Eugène did not neglect his duty in the watch shop as he had his law-office job. He was now twenty-one years old and knew he had to make his living in the world. Besides, he enjoyed working with his jeweler's tools. Magic was reserved for his leisure hours.

These were so few, however, that he did not progress as rapidly as he hoped. Then, quite by accident, he found a way to increase his practice time without neglecting his watchmaking.

One day he and his cousin Louis were closing their shop. When Jean Eugène turned around he saw a young man crossing the street. He had a thin piece of black wood in his hand and his fingers were rapidly drumming on it as he walked along.

Jean Eugène nudged his cousin. "Look!" he said. "Maybe he's a little crazy."

Louis Robert smiled. "Yes, he is, but not in the way you think. He is as crazy about being a violinist as you are to be a magician. That is the fingerboard of a fiddle he is carrying. He is practicing his fingering as he walks along."

"Oh!" Jean Eugène said. "That seems like a good idea."

"I suppose you will try the same thing," Louis said with a smile. "You could carry a rabbit in your hat and practice pulling it out as you walk along."

"You are making fun of me," the young man protested.

"Ah, my dear cousin, someday you will be a great watchmaker, for you have far more talent than either your father or myself. You have a magic way with tools. Is that not a greater talent than pulling odd things out of a hat?"

Jean Eugène did not argue, but he thought otherwise. He took a tip from the violinist. In his story of his life he said, "So whenever my hands were not otherwise engaged they slipped naturally into my pockets, and set to work with cards, coins, or some object. Thus, for instance, when out on errands my hands could be at work on both sides. At dinner, I often ate my soup with one hand while I was learning magic with the other."

About a year later Jean Eugène reached the point in his work in the shop where Cousin Louis could teach him nothing more. At this point Prosper Robert made arrangements for his son to work for M. Paul Norient in Tours. This was a break for the young watchmaker. M. Norient had a very high reputation as a maker of chronometers for ocean nagivation. Work with Norient et Cie would permit Jean Eugène to advance far beyond his father in the science of horology.

Jean Eugène liked people and people liked him. Before long he was like a member of the Norient family. It was no secret that M. Norient had his eye on the young man and that Mme. Norient was trying to decide which of her three daughers she would get him to marry.

Then, on July 25, 1828, there was another of those odd occurrences which seemed to indicate that Fate was fighting to turn Jean Eugène into the magician he dreamed of being.

He had gone to a party with the Norient family. When they came home Jeannette, the cook, had a ragout of beef waiting for them. The family tasted it and refused to eat it. Everyone felt it had an odd taste.

It tasted delicious to Jean Eugène, and he heartily ate two bowlfuls. About a half hour later he doubled up with dreadful cramps in his stomach. The alarmed family took him to his bed. A doctor was hastily summoned. He checked the young man and gravely told the worried Norients that it was food poisoning. Something had been wrong with the beef stew after all.

He prescribed a potion that eased Jean Eugène's terrible cramps. The young man fell into a feverish sleep. But during the night the violent pains returned and Jean Eugène woke up. His head hammered, and his skin was burning like fire.

He got up shakily from his bed and looked around him. He was so hot he could not think clearly. He walked down the back stairs without waking the Norients.

Outside, the breeze off the Loire River brought some relief from the fever's heat. He walked aimlessly, not knowing where he was going. The breeze on his face was pleasant, and walking helped ease the dreadful cramps.

The burning fever affected his brain to the point where he did not know what he was doing. Just at dawn he came to the post station where the daily coach was being hitched for the drive along the Loire from Tours to Orléans.

He stopped, too feverish to know where he was or what he was doing there. The coachman asked where he was going. Bewildered, Jean Eugène said that he wanted to go home.

"And where is your home?" the coachman asked.

The young man put his hand to his aching head. He tried to think. His head hurt too badly. It seemed to him that he had two homes, but all he could think of was Blois.

"Blois," the coachman repeated. "Ah yes, and that fair

town lies midway between here and Orléans. I can drop you there before nightfall. That is, of course, if you have the fare. Three francs, yes?"

Jean Eugène dug the money from his pocket. It was all he had. The coachman helped him inside, for he was too weak to make the step. He leaned back in the seat, his head rolled over in the corner. The pains were still gripping him unmercifully, but he was so exhausted that he slept in spite of them.

He awoke to the most terrible pain he had ever felt in his life. The coach was empty except for himself. The coachman was taking advantage of his light load to whip up his team. The road was rough, with deep ruts from a recent rain.

The coach bounced wildly, adding to Jean Eugène's torment. It became so bad he could not stand it any longer. He shouted for the coachman to stop, but the driver could not hear him above the creak of the coach and the pounding hooves of the four-horse team.

Weakly the young man leaned out the open window in the door, trying to shout up at the coachman. The coach reeled as it took a turn in the road. Jean Eugène was nearly thrown out. In the scramble, his knee hit the door latch. It swung open, dragging the young man with it. His feet hit the ground but he still clung to his grip on the swinging door.

He tried to scream to the coachman for help, but the words strangled in his throat. His fingers started to slip. He couldn't hold on any longer. He fell and the bouncing back wheels rolled just inches from his head as the coach raced on down the road.

It was days before the sick young watchmaker opened his eyes again. When he did he almost screamed. He was in a dark place. There was only a single candle, and a wind from somewhere caused its flame to flicker. This made the dark shadows seem alive.

But what scared him was the face bending down out of the shadows to look at him. It was a dark, slender, face, with a whisp of chin whiskers and a thin moustache. The eyebrows were heavy, the strange eyes piercing. There was some oil on the man's hair and the way the candlelight reflected off it made it seem to Jean Eugène that two tiny horns sprouted there.

"Oh, no!" the sick man whispered. "I knew I was bad, but I never thought I'd—"

He gulped, unable to go on. He shivered and stared in awe at the strange face above him.

"Perhaps I should speak to him first, master." Someone spoke from the shadows. "I think he believes you are the Evil One himself!"

The speaker came from the shadows. He was about Jean Eugène's age, but he was much shorter. His face was dark and impish.

"So!" he said. "You are awake at last. Seven days you have been sleeping. And do you know you would have slept forever and ever had it not been for the marvelous skill of my master, the Great Torrini!"

"You are a doctor, sir?" Jean Eugène asked weakly.

"Once I was, but that was many years ago, when I had another name," the strange man said. "Today I am just the Great Torrini. Not really great, of course. It is just that all magicians call themselves great. It is almost a rule."

"You are a magician!" Jean Eugène cried, struggling to sit up.

"Here!" Torrini said quickly, pushing the young man back on the bed. "You are not yet strong enough to move around so. You have been very sick."

"I know I was dying when I fell from the coach," Jean Eugène said. "You have saved my life, monsieur, and it is a debt that I must repay in some way."

"You repaid it when at last your fever broke and you opened your eyes. If it is true that I saved your life, and I pray to the good God that it is so, then you have saved mine. So we are even, my young friend."

"You are just saying that to make me feel better," the young man said.

A pained look passed across Torrini's face. "No," he said. "Once I took a life. Now if I have given one back, it will make me feel a little better."

He turned quickly away then, leaving his assistant, Antonio, to feed Jean Eugène some thin soup.

Torrini had gone off by himself to wander along the curving banks of the Loire. While he was gone, Antonio told Jean Engène the strange story of the unhappy magician's life.

Torrini's real name was Count Edmond de Grisy. Once he had been a wealthy doctor who dabbled in magic for a hobby. But as time went by he had become so interested in tricks that he gave up medicine and became a professional conjurer.

The count's most famous trick was catching in his teeth a bullet which was fired from a gun. Later he improved on the trick and called it "William Tell, Jr." In this version he fired the gun himself at an apple which his son held over his heart. After the gun was fired, the marked bullet was found in the apple. He named the trick after the famous tale of the Swiss archer who shot an apple from the head of his son.

It was a great success, until one day something went wrong. The trick was done by cleverly switching either the gun or the bullet, but on this fatal day Torrini got mixed up. He shot at the boy with the real shell.

He killed the boy and was placed in jail. It was an accident, and he was soon released. But while he was in prison, his wife died, and false friends stole his fortune. He came out a penniless, sorrowful man.

He turned away from everyone and everything he had known, took the name Torrini, and became a wandering magician. He had a horse and a wagon upon which was built a little house in which he and Antonio lived.

Jean Eugène could hardly wait for the brokenhearted magician to return. Then he poured out his heart's longings to Torrini.

"I want to be a magician more than anything else in the world," he said. "Can't I stay here with you and learn?"

"I cannot see how any man would wish to follow a profession which has brought me so much pain," Torrini said. "But I suppose you are as I once was. I gave up a name, a son, a wife, and a fortune to do my miserable tricks. If this be your wish, so be it. You can stay and starve with Antonio and me as long as you will."

The next day Jean Eugène wrote his parents a letter. He told them of his sickness, and that he would remain with Torrini until he had regained his strength. He did not yet have the courage to tell his father that he had decided to become a professional magician.

In a few days Torrini began Jean Eugène's education. The young men had a good foundation upon which to build. His finger practices had given him a passable palming and passing technique. What he needed most was instruction in stagecraft and stage manners.

This Torrini gave him before going into the intricate mechanical tricks.

First the magician had Jean Eugène do the little tricks he had performed at parties back in Blois.

"Why are you silent?" Torrini asked.

"I am trying to be a magician, not a lecturer," the young man replied.

"Ah! And there is where you are making a great mistake. A

magician's patter is his most effective tool. You must learn to talk, to tell jokes, to keep your audience amused, and at the same time to divert their attention from what your left hand is doing. I can sooner think of a blind artist as a dumb magician! Joke, brag, say outrageous things. In any other man it would be offensive, but people expect a magician to claim he is the greatest of the great."

In the days that followed, Jean Eugène learned trick after trick. Then one day he surprised Torrini. Only recently the old magician had taught him to do the Goldfish Bowl trick.

The way Torrini did it was to take a small fish bowl and cover it with a watertight oiled silk top, which kept the water from spilling out. The fish bowl was hidden under the magician's cloak.

Torrini would take a square of cloth and whip it in the air to show there was nothing hidden in it. Then, bringing it against his body, he would secretly lift the little goldfish bowl underneath. As he whipped the cloth away, his thumb would strip off the waterproof cover, which came away hidden under the cloth.

The effect was that he produced a bowl of swimming fish from nowhere.

"Now the secret of a good magician," Torrini told his rapt pupil, "is in the little touches. After you produce the fish from nowhere, be sure to let your hand shake a little. A bit of water will spill on the floor while you are acting as if you were trying to keep it from slopping over. Do you see why?"

"No, I don't," Jean Eugène admitted.

"Because it will make the trick seem even that more difficult. If the bowl is so full that even the slightest movement of the hand will cause it to slosh out, they will find it all the more amazing that you were able to drag it out of the air."

Torrini carefully explained that the entire secret of the trick was to get the waterproof cover off the bowl instantly and easily. If there was the slightest hesitation, it would give the secret away.

"That is why," Torrini said, "one must use a small fishbowl. It is impossible to get a large cover off quickly enough, even if one could make it tight enough to keep the water from spilling out."

As Jean Eugène stared at the cover, which was tightened about the lip of the bowl with a drawstring, the mechanical tinkering genius of the young man was already figuring out a new way to get the cover off quickly. While Torrini and Antonio were busy elsewhere, he quickly put together a gadget his active mind had figured out.

He had to wait several days before he could find all the parts and especially the large bowl he needed. Finally it was completed.

Then one evening, after Torrini had put on a show in a little village near Orléans, he asked the master to watch him try the Goldfish Bowl trick himself.

"If you want to produce something out of the air," Antonio said, "please make it a chicken. We didn't get enough money today to eat on tomorrow."

"Isn't it so," Torrini said sadly. "Forget the goldfish and produce some trout. Better still, make it a whale or two. We can eat on that for a week even with Antonio's appetite."

Jean Eugène only smiled at their banter. He quickly flourished his cloth and then stopped with an embarrassed grin. In his haste he had missed his grab at the hidden bowl.

Antonio laughed, but Torrini only said, "When you make a mistake, never look embarrassed. Smile confidently and act as if you planned it that way."

Jean Eugène took a deep breath and started again. This time he expertly hooked the bowl hidden under his cloak and removed the cover perfectly.

"Ah, splendid," Torrini said. "You did that very—what! What is this? How did you do that with such a large bowl?"

"Just a minute, until I spill a few drops of water like you told me," Jean Eugène said with a grin. Torrini's astonishment was the most splendid praise he had ever gotten in his life. It left him aglow.

"It is impossible!" Torrini said, staring accusingly at the bowl, which was twice the size of the one he used. "How did you do it?"

Jean Eugène showed him the gadget he had made. The waterproof cover was tightened about the lip of the bowl with springs. These were fastened to a metal crossbar which was pivoted so it would turn. When it was turned, it pulled the springs back, instantly releasing the cover. Then the entire clever gadget folded flat so it could remain hidden under the cloth and dropped out of sight while the audience's attention was on the mysteriously appearing bowl.

Torrini did not say anything. He stared speechless at the gadget. Jean Eugène became worried. He was afraid he had offended his master by topping his best trick. But finally Torrini smiled.

"Someday, my magician friend, you will be the greatest magician in France. You see, in anything one does it is not possible to stand still. One must improve and do more and more. Today, practically every magician is just repeating old tricks invented years ago and known to every conjurer. The Goldfish Bowl trick itself came to us from China, where it has been performed for centuries."

He was silent a moment and then continued. "But you have shown me tonight that you have the ability to improve and make your tricks better. This is the difference between being an average magician who calls himself great and one who really is great."

That night Jean Eugène went to bed in a rosy glow. In his

mind's eye he could see himself the great magician Torrini predicted.

He would not, however, have been so happy if he could have seen the mess he made of his first performance. It was so terrible that it drove him from the stage, and it was to be seventeen more years before he dared make a professional appearance again.

5. First Performance

By fall the little magician's caravan had wandered aimlessly through dozens of small villages. With each show, Jean Eugène's knowledge of the conjurer's art increased. He took part in the shows only as Torrini's assistant. On the stage he watched his master's movements and memorized his patter.

He was positive that he was now as good as Torrini, but when the chance came to prove it, he suddenly had doubts.

It happened that Torrini became ill. The little group was desperate for money. They needed medicine for the master. They needed food for themselves and forage for the horse.

Antonio and Jean Eugène talked things over while Torrini lay and tossed feverishly in his bed inside the wagon.

"We must put on the show ourselves," Antonio said. "We can see the mayor and get permission to use the town hall. We played here last year and everyone liked Torrini."

"Good," Jean Eugène said. "One of us had better stay with the master while the other goes to see the mayor."

"I'll arrange for the hall," Antonio said. "I am very good at crying, and I'll weep like a lost soul while I tell the mayor how our master's life depends upon this show. When I get done he'll let us have it for free!"

"Fine," Jean Eugène said. "While you are gone, I'll get the apparatus ready for you."

"Get it ready for yourself," Antonio replied. "You are the magician."

"Oh, no!" Jean Eugène cried, alarmed. "I've never—I mean —I can't!"

"I know you can't," Antonio said impatiently, "but you must just the same. I am a good assistant. I can sneak away the things the master drops out of the audience's sight, but my fingers are too clumsy to do the tricks."

"But it is different doing tricks in the parlor of your friends and doing them for people who pay to see you. I've never—"

"All it takes are nimble fingers and brains. You have the fingers, and I would tell you how smart I am if I were not so modest."

"But Antonio! I'll make a fool of myself."

"Would you rather be a fool, or have us all starve?"

"Oh, why did I leave my watchmaker's bench?" Jean Eugène said with a groan. "Why did I ever think I was a magician?"

"Because you were born to be one," Antonio replied. "Torrini says so."

"Well—if you really think—"

"I do not think, I know! You will be a great success. To-night a new magician will be born. Hail, the Great Robert!"

Antonio left to arrange for the hall, and Jean Eugène got the apparatus for the tricks ready. Some of his uneasiness left him. He was afraid he might have stage fright when he first got on stage alone for the first time. But strangely enough he had no fear at all once he made up his mind to go through with the act.

He opened with a little speech to gain the audience's sympathy. He apologized for his own appearance and told them about Torrini's sickness.

He opened the act with the Orange-Tree trick. He planted

a seed and covered it with a cone of paper. When he took it away, a tree had miraculously grown up. It had real fruit. This he plucked and gave to the audience.

The trick came off very well. It was just as Torrini had done it except that he did not give as many oranges away. They didn't have money enough to buy more.

He followed this with the Shower of Flowers. Once again he took a square of paper, which he rolled into a cone much like the one he had used to grow the orange tree. Then he poured from it a pile of flowers three times as large as the empty cone from which they came.

With each successful trick, Jean Eugène's confidence grew. He became excited, and this was his undoing.

His next offering was the Omelet-in-a-Hat trick. He borrowed a hat from a man in the audience, all the while keeping up a steady patter about having missed his dinner and how he hoped the audience would not mind if he took a moment out to cook himself an egg.

He held the egg up so the audience could see it. Then he broke it and dropped the contents into a small receptacle behind the hat, but did it so deftly that it seemed to the audience that the egg went into the crown of the upturned hat.

Grinning widely, Antonio brought him an outsize cooking spoon. While Jean Eugène went through a big show of stirring the egg in the hat, Antonio slipped away with the can with the broken egg.

He came back with a lighted candle which he sat on the *servante*, the magician's table, beside the upturned hat.

Jean Eugène proceeded to cook the omelet by holding the hat over the candle flame. He bent over and pretended to smell the cooking egg.

"Ah!" he said, rolling his eyes. "Delicious. Do you smell it?"

Suddenly his good humor turned to horror. He did smell something! He glanced down and saw that he had scorched the brim of the borrowed hat.

His patter froze in his throat. Antonio whispered frantically, "Keep talking! Quick! Turn out the omelet. Remember what Torrini told you. Act as if nothing had happened!"

Jean Eugène forced a shaky smile, but his mouth was so dry he could not get a single word out.

Antonio took up the patter. "And there, ladies and gentlemen," he cried as a well-done omelet seemed to drop from the hat. "You ladies whose husbands own hats can sell your cooking pots! Excuse me while I go cook myself an egg. I missed my supper, too!"

Grinning broadly, Antonio skipped off the stage with the scorched hat.

By this time the unhappy young magician had himself partly in hand. He started his next trick. It was a very ancient one known as the Rising Card.

Taking a deck of cards, he announced that he could make any card the audience cared to name rise from the deck simply by waving his wand over it.

Many voices spoke up, naming different cards. He waited until he heard someone ask for the Ace of Spades.

"Ah!" he said. "The gentleman in the third row has named the Queen of Hearts. So . . . but no! I notice that the nice lady in the second row has ask for the Ace of Spades. Now it would be ungallant to pass a lady. So with your permission, sir, it shall be the Ace!"

Then holding the deck in his right hand, he passed his magician's wand above it, commanding the ace to rise. Nothing happened!

Jean Eugène made a comical face and said to the cards in a loud whisper that could be heard throughout the hall, "Please! This is for a lady!"

He made an upward movement of the wand and the Obedient Card, as the trick was also known to magicians, rose slowly from the deck. It seemed to rise of its own accord, for the audience could not see the thin black thread which was fastened to the back of it with a bit of wax. The thread ran to the wand and Jean Eugène was gently pulling it up.

The trick was greeted with a ripple of applause, and for a moment the young magician forgot he still had to face the awful moment when he gave the ruined hat back to its owner.

"Now make my Queen of Hearts rise up!" cried the man in the third row.

"I—" Jean-Eugène tried to think of an excuse but failed.

It was impossible for him to make the card rise without attaching the invisible thread. This he could not do without going through the deck, finding the right card, attaching the thread with a bit of wax, and then tying the thread to the wand. He would have to leave the stage to do it. But to do that would destroy the realism of the trick. The audience would know he had left to rework the trick.

While he was fumbling around in his mind for an excuse, Antonio once again saved him. The Italian boy came trotting back on stage with a hat. He handed it to Jean Eugène. The young magician took it gratefully, happy for an excuse to lay down the now embarrassing deck of cards.

Antonio's quick whisper raised his alarm again when he remembered the accident to the hat.

"Just hand him the hat, but don't say anything. They always look inside to see if any egg remains there. He'll see a note I wrote."

Jean Eugène looked down at the piece of paper Antonio had placed in the hat. It read: "I ruined your hat. It was a regrettable accident. This hat is my own. Please take it as if it were your own and do not betray me to the audience. Tomorrow when the hatter opens, I will replace your ruined hat with a new one."

Jean Eugène looked at Antonio as if to say, "Will he do it?"

Antonio shrugged, silently saying, "I pray he will."

Feeling like a condemned man going to have his head chopped off, Jean Eugène walked to the edge of the stage and handed the hat back to its owner.

As Antonio predicted, the man looked inside the crown. Anxiously the two young men watched his face. They saw a blank look that slowly turned into a smile.

A wave of relief flashed over the worried young magician. His knees shook as he walked back to the *servante* to start his next trick.

But before he could pick up the empty can from which he intended later to pull a large French flag, the heckler in the third row jumped up. Once again he demanded that the magician cause the Queen of Hearts to rise from the deck of cards.

Jean Eugène looked at Antonio. For once the resourceful stage assistant could think of nothing. For just a second the young magician considered admitting he could not do the trick.

Always before when things had gone badly, Antonio had come to his aid. Now suddenly thrown on his own, Jean Eugène hesitated for only one bewildered second.

He had an active and inventive mind, but it worked only when pushed. A ripple of laughter at his obvious embarrassment was the push he needed. He was determined not to let this heckler make a fool of him.

Suddenly he had an idea.

"Yes," he said quickly. "I will have the queen rise for you."

He picked up the deck of cards and quickly shuffled through them. When he found the Queen of Hearts, he caught the card between the tips of two fingers. He was holding all the cards loosely and suddenly dropped them. Only the queen remained in his fingers.

Apologizing, he bent down on one knee to gather up the scattered deck. At the same time he slipped the queen up his sleeve. No one saw him. He got up feeling better.

He stepped off the stage, holding the deck of cards up where everyone could see it. Then he commanded the queen to rise. When nothing happened, he looked at the deck with a comical expression.

"Just like a woman," he said with a smile. "Ah! I know how to get her out. Queen! Come see that fur hat the lady in the third row is wearing!"

The men laughed and even the ladies smiled. Jean Eugène breathed easier. His lost confidence came back. He felt like laughing, he was so happy.

"Ah!" he said. "The queen did not come out! When a woman will not come to look at another woman's clothes, something is wrong."

He quickly riffled through the deck. He raised his head, a look of astonishment on his face. "There is no queen! No wonder she could not rise for us."

He handed the deck to the man who had insisted on seeing the queen rise. "Sir, would you look?"

The man verified the fact that the queen was indeed missing. This was when Jean Eugène should have retreated quickly and started another trick. But, flushed with confidence, he wanted to put a topper on his triumph.

"Now I know there was a Queen of Hearts in that deck when I came on this stage," he said. "Where can she be?"

He looked around him, seeking a place to find a card. His eyes lighted on a stern-faced old farmer, who looked back at him with a grumpy expression. It was the worst choice he could have made.

"Ah!" he cried. "Here is the wandering lady! Your pardon, m'sieur!"

He reached over and seemed to pick the lost card from under the old man's long beard. The audience broke into laughter. The man's face turned scarlet with rage.

He jumped to his feet. He shook his fist under the surprised nose of Jean Eugène.

"You—you young smart aleck!" he cried. "How dare you make a laughingstock of your elders! I should thrash you within an inch of your life."

He turned around and started to clump out of the hall, muttering, "No wonder the world is in such a sorry spot with young people going around making fun of their elders!"

The audience was amused by the old man's rage, but Jean Eugène was deeply hurt. He managed to finish the show, but it was a very unhappy young man who helped Antonio pack up the stage props to carry back to the wagon.

After buying a new hat to replace the ruined one, the two young men showed only a slight profit from their show.

Antonio gave Torrini an account of their troubles while Jean Eugène sat in red-faced embarrassment. He expected the old magician to upbraid him for being a dolt. To his surprise Torrini burst into loud laughter. It was the first and last time Jean Eugène heard the unhappy old man laugh.

Torrini sat up in bed. "I feel better already," he said. "Truly is it said that a good laugh is better than medicine. Do not look so sad, my fine friend. I do not laugh at you, but only because your troubles remind me of my first professional appearance on the stage. Now, my friend, smile. Often a bad beginning means a splendid finish!"

The profit from the show was enough to provide their supper anyway. After they ate, Torrini told Jean Eugène where he had made his mistakes.

"The burned hat—that is just one of those things. It could happen to anyone. But letting this man in the audience get the best of you was a bad mistake.

"Remember I told you that a magician's patter is the most important thing about an act. You must keep talking all the time. Never give anyone in the audience an opportunity to ask you anything. Keep talking and go immediately into your next act before they even have time to think about how you did the miracle they just saw."

Jean Eugène listened politely, but he had already made up his mind that he was not ready to be a magician. It was not his mistakes. These he understood and knew how to correct. What hurt him most was the angry old man's complaint that he was making fun of his elders.

"There will be more like him wherever I go," Jean Eugène told Antonio. "I am convinced that a young man will not succeed as a magician. Older people will resent him. No, my mind is made up. I am going back home and pick up my watchmaker's tools where I dropped them."

"But you can't do this!" Antonio protested. "You were born to be a magician. Torrini said so!"

Jean Eugène shook his head. "No, I do not intend to give up my dream of being a magician. But I will not again appear on the stage until I have gray hair. Then no one can say I am a young smart aleck making fun of his elders."

Antonio tried to argue. In the few weeks they had been together he had grown to love his friend. But Jean Eugène could not be talked into staying. As soon as Torrini was well again, he said good-bye.

"You go," Torrini said sadly, "but you will be back. You were born to be the greatest magician in the world, and no man can escape his destiny."

Jean Eugène was somewhat uneasy about the reception he

would get at home. His father surprised him. He was not angry at all.

"So!" he said after welcoming his son. "You ran away to be a magician, but you found out that it is no life for an ambitious young man, eh?"

"Oui, Papa."

"Now I have a little confession of my own to make to you. You see, many, many years ago, when I was your age, I ran away from my workbench, too! I wanted to be a sailor. Now if there is anything more foolish than being a magician, it is being a sailor!

"Well, I made one trip on the sea and it taught me that the best place for me was at my own workbench. So now you have learned the same thing. You can now work hard and become a very great watchmaker. It was my great dream that you should be a lawyer, but since that is impossible, I want you to be the best watchmaker in France."

"I will try, Papa," Jean Eugène said.

"And I will help you this one last time. The rest is up to you. Visiting in Blois today is M. Houdin, the famous Parisian watchmaker. He and I were apprentices together here in Blois. I have asked him to take you into his shop!"

"Oh, Papa, this is wonderful!"

"I think so too. There is a young people's party tonight for his daughter. I have not seen her, but even if she is as homely as a mud fence, be nice to her. She is the apple of Houdin's eye. We must do nothing to offend him until you are safely in his shop!"

"I will try," Jean Eugène said.

6. The Prefect of Police Turns a Trick

Jean Eugène arrived at the party a little late. As he came in, a friend he had not seen in a long time stopped him.

"Where have you been?" his friend Marcel asked. "I heard you had gone off to Paris to be married."

"You heard wrong," Jean Eugène said. "I shall never marry. I am convinced that only an idiot does something like that."

"After all, your father got married," Marcel said with a smile.

"Yes, but girls must have been different in those days."

"Oh, is *that* so!" mocked a very pretty voice.

Jean Eugène turned in surprise to see the prettiest girl he had ever seen.

"You, sir, are the one who is an idiot!" she snapped, her black eyes flashing fire. She swept off with an angry toss of her brown curls.

"Who in the world is that spitfire?" Jean Eugène asked.

"That is Josie Cecile Eglantine Houdin, our guest of honor."

"Oh, no!" Jean Eugène said. "Oh, I hope she doesn't tell her father."

As it happened, Josie did not tell her father that the young man he was taking on as an apprentice thought that only idiots got married. The day when he reported to her father's shop, Jean Eugène apologized to Josie for what he had said at the party. She received his apology coldly. He was sure that the pretty girl disliked him. He tried to keep out of her sight, but somehow he continually kept running into her. This embarrassed him at first, but after a while he was making excuses to be near her. Within a few weeks he decided that he had been wrong and that only an idiot would not want to marry such a lovely girl. He proposed and was accepted.

M. Houdin was pleased to have the son of his old friend for a son-in-law. After the wedding he asked the young man to take the Houdin name, since he hoped that someday Jean Eugène would inherit the Paris business. With his own father's permission, he received legal authority to change his name to Jean Eugène Robert-Houdin.

And so was born the name which he was to make world famous in a profession he thought then had been put behind him forever.

The years passed swiftly. By 1838, Jean Eugène Robert-Houdin was the father of four children and had an excellent reputation for his inventions and automata. However, none of them seemed to make him much money.

One was quite clever. It was an alarm clock that struck a flint and steel which lighted a candle for lazy sleepers.

Then he had an idea that he could make a lot of money with an automata show. He built about thirty clever figures that operated by clockwork. There were clowns jumping through hoops, a little trapeze artist, a large model of the hunter shooting a rabbit he had originally made for his father's snuffbox, and many others.

Unfortunately it cost more to make the little figures than he made with his show. This venture left him badly in debt.

Then, one late spring day, as he was returning from delivering some chronometers near Notre Dame Cathedral, on the Île de la Cité, a sly voice spoke up behind him.

"Don't give *that* one your hat, sir, for he'll scorch it with his omelet making!"

Jean Eugène whirled around to face a grinning Antonio. Ten years had passed since he left Torrini's magic wagon, but they had done little to Antonio except make his clothes a little ragged.

The delighted watchmaker threw his arms around his old friend.

"Antonio!" he cried so loudly that people stopped a block away to stare at him. "Oh, I am so glad to see you. How is Torrini?"

The smile faded from Antonio's face. "The master died six years ago," he said.

"Oh," Jean Eugène said. His own gaiety vanished.

For a while the two old friends walked along the bank of the Seine talking about the old magician they had both loved so well.

"There has not been a day since I left you that I have not thought of our happy times as wandering magicians," Houdin told his friend.

"The master talked of you all the time," Antonio said. "We often wondered where you were and what you were doing. Do you know what he said?"

"No," Jean Eugène said.

"Many times I heard him say the same thing: 'I don't know where he is or what he is doing, but I do know he is wasting his time if he is not doing tricks. God intended for him to be a magician.' "

Houdin smiled sadly. "I admit I have not forgotten my dream. I still practice when I can spare time from my work. I plan new tricks all the time, and I never miss a magic performance in Paris. Someday, Antonio, someday—"

"Why not today?" Antonio cried. "This minute! Together you and I will present the greatest wonders any villagers ever saw!"

Houdin laughed. "Not so fast, my friend. I am not yet ready. I have very sad proof that the public will not accept a young magician. I must wait until my hair is gray."

"That is foolish! How can you let the memory of one crotchety old man keep you from what you want to do. Come! We will buy a horse and be off to the provinces!"

"Will there be enough room in the wagon for my wife and four children?" Houdin asked with a smile.

"Oh! I'm afraid they would not fit in well with the gypsy life of a magician," Antonio admitted.

"But does a magician have to live a gypsy life?" Houdin asked, his excitement growing. "I don't think so. What I want to do is to build a theater here in Paris where I will put on my magic show every night."

"No, no," Antonio said. "There are only a few tricks. People will get tired if they see them over and over. The only way a magician can keep going is to move all the time, catch a new audience each night. Then the tricks will always seem new."

"I want my own magic theater."

"You'll starve!"

"I don't think so. It will be something completely new. There is nothing like it in France anywhere. Some theaters here in Paris use magicians to entertain between acts, but nowhere is there a place that shows only magic."

"You'll be making a mistake," Antonio said positively.

"The trouble with magic is that nobody takes it seriously," Houdin said. "I want to make people look upon a magician as an artist, the same as they do an opera singer. I'll throw away the funny loud suits. I'll perform in a dress suit. I'll throw out the candles put up to shine in the audience's eyes and make it hard for them to see the poor technique of the magician. I'll not be a clown. I'll be an artist!"

"And a starving one. No, Jean Eugène, it will not work. Come with me. Let us revive Torrini's act. I tried to carry it on after he died, but my fingers are too clumsy."

"I'm sorry, Antonio. Right now I must work to feed my family. Later, when I have saved some money, I'll have my own magic theater. Until then, I make watches."

The two old friends parted a short time later. Antonio went in search of someone to help him develop an act for the country towns. Houdin went back to his tools.

The years passed. At last there was a touch of gray in his hair, but still he wasn't ready. This time it was money. Somehow, there was only enough to feed his growing family. He could never scrape up enough to build the tricks his inventive mind sketched.

He went to see every magician who came to Paris, and every one of them disappointed and angered him. He was positive that it was possible to make the public treat magicians as something besides mountebanks.

But there seemed nothing he could do about it. He hid his disappointment and continued work on a mechanical man which, when its clockwork was wound, could draw pictures and write words.

Before this marvelous automaton was completed, Houdin showed it to Count de l'Escalopier, a nobleman who was also deeply interested in magic.

The count was so impressed by the dog drawn by the still incomplete machine that he asked Houdin to build him a gadget to catch a thief.

"Someone is stealing things from my desk drawer," the count said. "I have laid all sorts of traps, but have been unable to catch the thief."

"I can build a gun into the drawer so he will shoot himself when he pulls it open," Jean Eugène suggested.

"Oh, no!" the count said. "I don't want to kill anyone. The nature of my business makes it necessary for me to keep rather large sums of money about the house. I just want to protect my property. Regular locks don't seem to work."

"If your Grace will come back tomorrow, I will have something," Houdin said.

And true to his word, when the count returned the next day, Jean Eugène had built what he called a "detector lock." When the drawer was opened by one who did not know the combination, a little iron cat's claw leaped out and scratched the thief's hand.

After that it was only necessary for the count to inspect the hands of his servants to find the one who had been stealing from him.

He was so delighted that he offered Houdin a large reward. The inventor refused. After an argument, the count said, "Then let me lend you ten thousand francs for that theater you have been talking about for years."

Jean Eugène hesitated. He had refused the reward because he did not feel he had earned it. He had been asked to do a job and had been paid his regular fee. It smacked of charity to take a reward he felt was unnecessary.

But the loan was something else. He would not be taking something for nothing. He could repay it all with interest.

"Monsieur," he said, "I will accept the loan with gratitude."

"Splendid!" the count said. "And I will be expecting that extraordinary show you have been promising to do for years."

After he made the deal, Jean Eugène had a few moments of doubt. He was forty years old, and it had been seventeen years since he had taken Torrini's place in the show at Aubusson. The memory of that awful experience still made him feel uneasy. He suddenly felt stage fright before he even got on stage.

"Suppose I fail again?" he asked himself.

The thought of losing the entire ten thousand francs made him shiver. He could see himself working for the rest of his life to pay off the enormous debt.

As the theater neared completion, however, his enthusiasm returned. He worked night and day. During the daylight hours, he helped remodel the stage. At night he worked with his tricks until he fell asleep from exhaustion.

The theater was built on the second floor of an apartment house, the Palais Royal. He rented two suites and removed the wall between them. At one end was the stage, and the rest was divided into a pit, stalls, and boxes. It seated only 180 people, but it was a complete theater despite its small size.

He fitted up the stage like a palace drawing room and announced that he would keep his promise to appear in a dignified dress suit. Other magicians said he was crazy. Their flowing robes and quaint costumes were not just for show. They served to hide things they did not wish the audience to see. They said Houdin would find it impossible to do very many tricks in a dress suit, under which little could be hidden.

He felt, however, that this would make his tricks appear more difficult to the audience. Also he was determined to appear more dignified than the clowning jesters who did most of the magic tricks.

The theater was completed in June, 1845, and named the Robert-Houdin Theater. For a while he considered calling himself Torrini II but finally decided to use his own name because it was so well known from his work with mechanical toys.

A week before the first show, he put up posters around Paris. They read like this:

THURSDAY, JULY 3, 1845
First Representation
of
The Fantastic Soirées of
Robert-Houdin

Among the Novel Experiments Will Be

The Cabalistic Clock	The Obedient Card
The Orange-Tree Trick	The Miraculous Fish Bowl
The Mysterious Bouquet	The Fascinating Owl
Pierrot in the Egg	The Pastry Cook

To Commence at Eight o'Clock

Price of Places: upper boxes, 1 franc 50 centimes; stalls, 3 francs; boxes, 4 francs; dress circle, 5 francs.

On June 25, Houdin gave a private performance for his friends to check on the smoothness of his act. It was a great success. The rich stage setting made his ordinary tricks seem more wonderful than they really were. For the first time, magic was presented on stage as a big production instead of in the streets or as a between-acts show.

Although he had a good reception, Houdin was still nervous about his first professsional performance. Everyone told him that he had nothing to worry about, but he could not shake the feeling that disaster awaited him on stage.

As it happened, he was right and they were wrong. Trouble was coming, although it did not wait until he got on stage.

A few days before the opening, Houdin was in the theater helping tack down a new strip of carpet on the stage. A policeman came clumping up the stairs, asking to see the manager of the little theater.

"Oui, m'sieur," Houdin said. "I am the manager. Is there something I can do for you?"

"You are opening a theater?" the policeman asked.

"But yes! My first show is Thursday."

"Ah, yes," the policeman said. "And may I see your license, monsieur?"

"My license for what?" Houdin asked.

"To open a theater. It is required in Paris. You have one, of course."

"Of course not! I didn't even know one was needed."

"Then I regret, monsieur, that it will be impossible for you to open your performances on Thursday."

"It is impossible for me not to open!" Houdin cried heatedly. "I have put out the posters. I have told everyone. I have spent ten thousand francs of someone else's money. I must open!"

"I regret to inform you that if you open you will close in jail. The law is the law."

"But I never heard of such a silly law! Since I didn't know about it, naturally you will understand why I must be permitted to go on with my act."

"There is nothing silly about the law, Monsieur Houdin, as you will find out if you try to put on a show without a license. It makes no difference whether you knew about the law or not."

"This is tyranny!" Houdin cried, his outraged excitement growing. "I'll write a letter to the king himself!"

"Don't you think it would be easier to get a license?" the policeman said, amused at Houdin's anger.

"How do I get one?"

"You make an application to the city council. They will consider and decide maybe yes and maybe no."

"How long does that take?" Jean Eugène asked.

"The next meeting will be on July fifteenth."

"But I can't wait that long!" Houdin cried. "I will see Count de l'Escalopier! I am sure he can help me."

He rushed across Paris to the count's home, but found that his friend had gone to Bordeaux. He was in despair by the time he got back to his own house.

In the morning he was told that he might get a temporary permit from the Prefect of Police. He tried to make an appointment with the prefect but was turned back by an assistant.

Dejected and certain that he had failed once again, Houdin returned home.

"It is a terrible thing to want something so badly all your life and then to have it stolen from you just at the moment when it seemed so sure," he told his wife.

"But it is only a few weeks' delay," she said. "You will have your theater yet."

"No," he said bitterly, "the theater cost two thousand francs more than I had. I borrowed this much from the bank. I gave a note payable in two weeks. I was sure I could make that much profit. If I do not pay, the bank will take the theater. I will owe the count ten thousand francs and have nothing. I must open on time or all is lost."

"Perhaps there is some other way," Mme. Houdin said. "You have done so much work for so many people. Isn't there someone who can help you? Didn't you repair a watch for the prefect? I seem to remember something about him."

"No, it was a striking clock for his brother, M. Delessert. I remember it quite well, for no one else in Paris could repair it."

Suddenly Houdin's face brightened. "Now that I recall it, this job was a very difficult one. There were some little clock-work figures made like ballet dancers on top of the clock. It was a favorite of M. Delessert's daughter. He was quite anxious to have it repaired, and complimented me highly on my work."

"Perhaps he would speak to his brother the Prefect of Police," Mme. Houdin suggested.

"I have already thought of that, madame," Houdin said happily. "Where is my coat? I will run over and see him right now."

"But, my husband! It is one o'clock in the morning!"

"Oh, I don't mind going out so late for such an important purpose," Jean Eugène said, struggling into his coat.

"I am not thinking of you. I am wondering how M. Delessert will feel about you waking him from his sleep to ask a favor."

"Oh!" Houdin said, and then grinned sheepishly. "Perhaps it would be better to wait until morning."

The next day he presented himself to the prefect's brother. M. Delessert was a large man with small, shrewd eyes. He sat fingering his huge gray moustache while Houdin talked.

When Jean Eugène had finished, M. Delessert spread his big hands in a gesture of helplessness.

"Ah, m'sieur," he said, rolling his eyes sadly. "I wish I could help you. But really, my brother the prefect does not permit anyone to tell him how to conduct his business. I would most gladly speak to him, but it would only enrage him. It would make him angry with me and do no good for you."

Jean Eugène swallowed hard. He had built his hopes high on the feeling that the prefect's brother could help him. Now he was almost drowned in the wave of disappointment. He got slowly to his feet.

"I apologize for taking your time," Houdin said, picking up his hat.

"Not so fast, Monsieur Houdin," the other man said.

He shifted around, making the chair creak with his great weight.

"I want to help, of course. It just occurred to me. No! I will not suggest it."

"Please do, m'sieur."

"Well, I just happened to remember. I am giving a garden party tomorrow night. My brother will be there. Now if you should just happen to come yourself and put on a show for my guests, he would see you. If the show impresses him—who knows, monsieur. Perhaps he would consider your request for a theater license!"

Houdin swallowed his anger. He knew that M. Delessert was only trying to get free entertainment for his party. Since it was the only way Houdin could meet the Prefect of Police, however, he agreed to do his act.

He rushed home to prepare for it. Mrs. Houdin pointed out that he was working harder to do an act free than when he was paid.

"That is true," he said. "But I must have everything perfect. Our whole future depends upon opening our theater. I must impress the prefect."

Because the show was outside, some of his best acts could not be used. Then the act he was depending upon failed to work out. This was the Dead Pigeon trick in which the magician comes on stage with a white bird perched on his finger. He cuts off the bird's head. He holds up the separated head and body so the audience can see that it is truly dead.

Then a cloth is thrown over the headless body, the wand is waved, and the cloth is removed. The "dead" bird is miraculously restored to life.

"This is terrible," Houdin cried. "This miserable bird will not do its part!"

"What are you trying to do, Father?" asked Émile, Houdin's twelve-year-old son.

"This faker Bosco does this trick by cutting off the bird's head. Then under cover of the cloth, he switches the dead bird for a live one. But I will not kill a bird to do a trick.

"Yesterday in the park I saw a sleeping bird. It gave me an idea. When a bird sleeps it tucks its head under its wing. From the audience this looks as if the bird had no head.

"So I bought this bird. I had a wooden head and neck carved and painted to look like the real thing. Now I am trying to train this stubborn creature to tuck its head under its wing when I tap it with the wand."

"Won't he do it?" Émile asked.

"No! He will ride on my finger. He will stay still when I tell him, but he refuses to act like he is asleep."

"Why don't you really chop his head off, like Bosco does? That would serve him right."

"I feel like it," Houdin said angrily. "But I cannot be so cruel."

"Then what are you going to do?"

"I suppose I must use some other trick. I don't know what I can do. It must be something unusual. Something so—so dramatic, so surprising that the audience will gasp. Now what in the world can I do?"

"What about your Fascinating Owl?" Mrs. Houdin said. "I think that is—"

"No, no!" Houdin said. "It is too large to take to the party. That trick can be done only on a theater stage. That is what my trouble is. I can do any number of simple tricks at the party, but I must have something which they have not seen other magicians do before. I must shock them. Surprise them. Mystify them. Don't you understand, madame? I must prove to the prefect that I am a better magician than any other conjurer in Paris!"

"Make me disappear like you did in the theater the other night," Émile suggested.

"No, son," Houdin said. "In the theater we have a trapdoor in the stage through which you can slip when I hold the cloth up to hide you from the audience. At M. Delessert's party I will be outside on the grass. There will be no hole for you to crawl into."

"I am sure you will be a great success. You worry too much," Mme. Houdin said.

"Who wouldn't worry when he is in danger of losing ten

thousand francs and disgracing himself besides?" Houdin said indignantly.

"I still think you should make me disappear, Father," Émile said.

"I would like to right now," his father said. "And I think I will. Up to bed with you, young man!"

"But I didn't mean—"

"But I do. And not one more word from you. I have work to do. And—wait! Wait! Seeing your mother's black velvet gown in the candlelight gives me an idea! Maybe—just maybe, my son, I will make you disappear after all!"

He extinguished the gaslights and set up candles as they would be at the garden party. Then he hung up a large square of black velvet for a backdrop.

"Now, madame," he said to his wife, "if you will just step from the room for a moment—"

"I will not!" she said. "I want to see how you do it. After all, I know it is just a trick. Don't try to fool me! I have been watching your tricks and helping you with them for years and years and years!"

"Please," Houdin said wearily. "I am not trying to fool you. I just want you to come back after I set up the stage. I want you to see the trick as M. Delessert's guests will see it. If it looks real to you, it will look real to them."

"But don't try to keep any secrets from me! I want to know how you did it!"

"*If* I do it," Houdin replied.

As soon as she left the room, he hung another, smaller piece of black velvet in front of the larger backdrop. Then he stepped back to look at the black curtain from the distance at which his audience would see it. The soft black pile of the velvet killed reflections, and the two pieces of material blended together so that the two looked like a single backdrop.

"Excellent! Wonderful! Magnificent!" Houdin cried.

Émile, my son, you are going to vanish right before the eyes of the party guests!"

He was shaking with excitement as he took Émile over and showed him exactly what to do. He knew that when vanishing acts are done on the stage, the audience suspected that trapdoors are used. But people at the party would know traps were impossible there. This would make the trick even more astounding to his audience.

Satisfied at last, Houdin called his wife back into the room. "Now watch closely, madame," he said. "I want to know if anything about the trick does not look real."

He walked over to Émile, who stood with his back to the velvet drop. In his hands was his scarlet-lined black cape. He draped it over one arm and put his hand on Émile's shoulder.

"You are going on a far journey into the unknown, son," he said in a sad voice. "Are you afraid?"

"A little, sir," the boy replied.

"Then you are very brave," Houdin said, rehearsing the patter which would accompany the act. "It is a very dangerous, very mysterious journey you will make. Are you ready?"

"I am ready, sir," Émile said, forcing a brave smile.

"In that case . . ." Houdin turned to face his audience of one person.

"*Voilà!* Now you see him. . . !"

He whipped the scarlet-lined cape up so it hid Émile for a brief second.

"*Voilà!* Now you *don't!*"

He dropped the cape, and the boy had disappeared!

He looked sharply at his wife to see her reaction. It was all he hoped for. Mrs. Houdin jumped to her feet.

"Why—why—it's just like *magic*," she cried.

"What do you mean, just like magic!" Houdin said indignantly. "It *is* magic."

"Oh, stop that, Jean Eugène!" Mrs. Houdin said. "You

know what I mean. It looked so real it did not seem like a trick at all."

"Well," Houdin said, smiling happily, "that is but half the trick. I must bring him back, you know! Now watch closely, madame, you see there is nothing up my sleeve! So he cannot be there!"

The magician turned and the cape whirled through the air. When he dropped it, Émile stood there smiling at his mother.

Mrs. Houdin clapped her hands. "Oh, Jean Eugène," she cried. "It is a wonderful trick."

"I'd like it better if I *really* disappeared," Émile said.

"And I suggest we all disappear to bed," Houdin said. "It is late and there is so much to do tomorrow."

"I'm not leaving this room until you tell me how you did that," Mrs. Houdin said.

The magician sighed. "If you insist. But wonderful tricks don't seem so wonderful after their secrets are revealed."

"Of course, you are right," she said. "Forget that I asked. You are a real magician, and Émile actually vanished!"

Houdin's act at the garden party was an outstanding success. The Prefect of Police was greatly impressed. He came over to talk to the magician when it was over. Houdin quickly told him about the trouble he was having getting a license.

"But you are a magician," the police chief said jokingly. "Surely all you have to do is wave your wand and—*voilà!*—there will be a license!"

"I am afaid, your Excellency, that it is not so easy," Houdin replied.

Another guest interrupted to ask Houdin about the vanishing act. The magician answered the man's questions and then turned back to the prefect.

But he had gone.

Houdin's shoulders sagged. He felt a wave of sick despair. All his work had gone for nothing. The police chief had only made a joke about Houdin's troubles and had gone away. He struggled to hide his disappointment behind a brave smile as other guests came up to talk to him.

Then, just before the guests started leaving, the prefect came back to Houdin.

"Did you know that I am also a magician, Monsieur Houdin?" he said.

"No, I did not, sir," Jean Eugène replied.

"And I might even be a better one than you! I will bet you one franc that I can do a magic trick that you cannot do."

Houdin smiled sadly. "I fear I do not even have a single franc in my pocket. So I cannot bet."

The prefect turned to his brother. "Loan our friend a franc," he said. "I am going to win this bet!"

M. Delessert smiled and took a coin from his pocket. The prefect bowed to Houdin and took a piece of folded paper from his jacket. He handed it to Jean Eugène. The magician opened it, wondering what the trick was. He expected something to jump out of the paper. Instead he saw only a few words written in ink.

They said, "This is our permission for M. Houdin to open the Robert-Houdin Theater in the Palais Royal. François Delessert."

He looked up, surprised. The police chief chuckled. "See," he said. "I win the bet. You said yourself that you could not wave your wand and produce a theater license. But I have done so!"

Houdin bowed to the prefect. "Excellency," he said, "you are right. This is the most delightful trick in the history of magic. I am grateful."

7. Emile's Amazing Second Sight

With this permission, Jean Eugène Robert-Houdin opened his conjurer's theater to the public on the night of July 3, 1845. It was a success, but not what he had wanted.

He had no trouble filling the 180 seats every night. He was making as much money as he had as a watchmaker and was able to pay back a little of his debt to Count de l'Escalopier.

Still he was not satisified. His act was better than that of other magicians. He produced a bigger bowl of goldfish. He made Émile vanish from a raised platform, so the audience could see that he was not using a trapdoor in the floor. His stage setting was better. And his working in a dress suit made the tricks seem even more impossible.

Regardless of this, he was only doing the same tricks they did. Better, yes, but still the same things. There was not enough difference to give him the worldwide fame he wanted. Not knowing the technical excellence of his work, the public did not realize fully the superiority of Houdin's craft. Other magicians knew it, however, and they came to watch his show and copy his new methods.

During this time, he continued to work with his automata, and finally completed his mechanical figure that could write and draw.

This technical marvel consisted of a young man dressed in

the court costume of the days of Louis XVI. He sat in a chair before a beautifully carved writing table. His hand held a pen that Houdin dipped in ink before starting the complex clockwork machinery inside. On the back, hidden from view, were a half-dozen springs which Houdin would press to cause the figure to write answers to questions.

Sometimes these were straight answers. Sometimes the machine would draw a picture in reply. There was a tiny clock inside, whose hands controlled a series of gears that could cause the mannequin to write the exact time when asked.

When asked, "What is faithfulness?" Houdin could press the center spring and a series of other gears would cause the tiny hand to draw the figure of a dog.

Houdin exhibited the mannequin at the Paris Quinquennial Exposition and was awarded a silver medal.

One of the visitors to the exposition was the famous American showman P. T. Barnum. Thirty-five years later, Barnum wrote in his autobiography about Houdin:

> When I was abroad in 1844, I went to Paris to attend the exhibition that is held every five years. I met and became well acquainted with a celebrated conjurer Robert-Houdin, but who was not only a legerdemain performer, but a mechanic of absolute genius who displays wonderful ability and ingenuity.
>
> I bought the best automaton he displayed. I paid a good round sum for this most ingenious little figure which was an automatic writer and artist. I took this curiosity to London, and then sent it across the Atlantic to my American museum where it attracted great attention from the people and the press.

Barnum came often to the theater to watch Houdin's act, and was a guest at the magician's home. Here he was particularly astounded by Houdin's use of electricity.

Soon after the Barnum visit, Houdin made another of those lucky discoveries that helped him out all through his life. Sometimes some ordinary little thing would attract his attention, and his inventive mind would immediately see a way he could make use of it in his magic. The sight of the sleeping bird made him think of a new way to make the "dead" pigeon come back to life. Mme. Houdin's black velvet gown inspired the Vanishing Person trick. And now a children's game had given him the idea for an act so amazing it was to make him the most famous magician in the world.

One rainy afternoon about a year after he had opened the Robert-Houdin Theater, Jean Eugène came home to find his children playing in the living room. Before going upstairs to work on a new trick he was planning, Houdin paused for a moment to watch Émile and his younger brother, Prosper, at their game.

Émile had a blindfold over his eyes and Prosper ran around the room touching first one object and then another. Each time he would shout, "What is this?"

Émile would guess. When he guessed correctly, the two boys would change places.

Houdin smiled and started up the stairs. Halfway to the top he stopped. A peculiar expression crossed his face. He turned and looked back at the laughing boys. Suddenly he gave an excited cry and started running down the steps.

"Children! Children!" he shouted.

Mrs. Houdin came running from the next room. "Is something wrong?" she cried in alarm.

"Oops!" Houdin cried as he bumped into a chair and almost fell. In his excitement he had failed to see it.

"Are you hurt, Father?" Émile cried, running over to him.

"Now see what you've done!" Prosper cried. "You spoiled our game just when it was my time to be 'it.' "

Houdin laughed delightedly and swept both boys up in his arms. "Children! Children!" he cried. "You have just made your father the most famous magician in the world!"

He dropped them back to the floor. "Back to your game. I have work to do!"

He rushed up the stairs, leaving his surprised family staring after him.

Émile started to follow, but his mother stopped him. "Do not bother your father when he has an idea," she said.

"I won't speak to him," the boy replied. "I just want to listen outside the workshop door."

"Very well," she said, "but do not go inside."

Shortly he came back downstairs. He had a puzzled expression.

"Mother," he said, "Father is in that room talking to *me* when I'm not even there!"

"Well, don't be alarmed. He is just practicing what he will say to you later," she replied.

Then, with her curiosity getting the better of her, she said, "What was he saying?"

"He said, 'Émile, what does this gentleman have in the pocket of his vest?' How do I know? I don't know the gentleman. And even if I did, how would I know what is in his pocket?"

"I really don't know either, my dear. But your father is a very great man. I'm sure he will find a way to tell you."

In the workshop Houdin was rapidly pacing the floor. He kept talking to himself, stopping now and then to make some notes on a piece of paper.

Finally, with the basic idea firmly in mind, Houdin extinguished the light. He walked to the window and watched the stars fade from the sky as dawn began to light the rooftops of Paris.

The next day he started to work with Émile on the trick which became famous as Second Sight. They worked together for two months before Houdin decided that they were ready for a public act.

In great excitement he had a poster put up in front of the theater which read:

"M. Robert-Houdin's son, who is gifted with a marvelous second sight, will have his eyes covered with a thick bandage. Then he will name any object presented to him by the audience!"

After his regular acts were over, Houdin presented Second Sight at the close of the show. He walked down into the audience while Émile, heavily blindfolded, remained seated on the stage.

Stopping beside a man in the audience, Houdin asked to select some object from his pocket. The man pulled out a penknife such as gentlemen once used to cut quills for writing pens.

"Émile!" Houdin shouted across the room to the boy on the stage. "What is the gentleman holding in his hand?"

"It is a penknife," the boy replied.

Houdin was surprised when there was no applause. He thought maybe the audience did not understand that the boy was instantly naming something it was impossible for him to see. He carefully explained this to them before repeating the trick from another side of the room. This time Émile correctly named a pearl pin worn by a lady.

Still the audience was not impressed by the new trick. After two more attempts, Houdin closed the show for the night.

He could not understand why the trick had failed. He discussed it with a friend the next day.

"Someone did a trick something like it some time ago," he was told. "The secret got out. He was using an accomplice who watched with field glasses from a secret window in the theater. He could see what object the person was holding. This secret watcher had a speaking tube that ran to the stage, and could tell the blindfolded medium what he was supposed to name."

For a while Houdin considered dropping Second Sight, but decided to give it more of a trial. At the next performance he explained to the audience how the trick had been done before. To assure them that no secret watcher with field glasses could spy out the secret, he had Émile's chair raised so they could see that no speaking tube ran up him. Then he had each person hold the object in his cupped hands so it would be impossible for a watcher to see it.

These changes created more interest, but still the trick did not produce the amazement Houdin had hoped for. He was just about to close the show for the night when a man stood up in the audience.

"I was here last night," he said. "I was not satisfied with your Second Sight and came back tonight to make things more difficult for you."

"Excellent!" Houdin said. "Here, take my handkerchief and hold it over the objects so that no one but you, another witness of your own choosing, and I can see them."

When this was done, Houdin said to Émile, "What is the object upon which the gentleman has placed his index finger?"

"It is an ancient Roman coin."

"Is there a name for it?"

"It is called the Widow's Mite."

"And why is it so called?"

"Because it is the coin in the Bible."

The owner of the coin looked startled. Then he touched the second article he had brought.

"Émile, the gentleman is touching what article with his finger?"

"It is a French franc coin."

"Very well, my son, and can your marvelous second sight, which can see through the thick bandages over your eyes, tell us the date stamped on the coin?"

"The date of the coin . . . Wait, Father, let me see. . . . The figures are so very small. . . ."

"Yes, yes, but if your second sight is real and no trick, you will be able to tell us!" Houdin said.

"One—eight—four—" He stopped and looked confused.

"Yes, yes," Houdin said.

"One—eight—four—four."

"Why—why, that is correct!" the man cried. "I don't see how he could possibly see those numbers. Why, I can hardly see them myself, and I am holding the coin in my hand!"

The man next to him, whom he had chosen as a witness, was just as excited. "By Jove! I would not have believed it! Even if I had paid ten francs for my ticket tonight, I would consider them well spent. This is marvelous!"

Their enthusiasm was contagious. It swept the theater. All over the hall people were on their feet, wanting Émile to name things for them.

The happy magician kept the theater open for another hour, long past the usual closing time. The next day his de-lighted audience spread the word of the marvelous Second Sight around Paris. Crowds jammed the little theater and many had to be turned away.

One night those who could not get tickets became unruly and forced their way in, taking seats from the ticket holders who had not yet arrived. Mme. Houdin suggested that they call the police, but the magician refused. He went to the box office himself and returned the money to those who held tickets but could not get in. Then he went back inside and gave a free performance to those who had stolen their seats. They were willing to pay at the end, for they had had no intention of stealing in the first place. It was just that the show had become so famous and they wanted so badly to see it. The small size of the theater made it impossible for everyone who wanted to see the performance to get in. Houdin refused the money.

The next day all Paris heard about the show that was so marvelous that people practically broke down the door to get in.

Houdin did not want any more riots by people who could not get into his theater, so he agreed to put on shows in larger places. These extra shows were held each night after he finished his performance in his own Robert-Houdin Theater. It meant finishing the first performance at ten thirty, and rushing by horse cab across Paris to the other theater, where his next show began at eleven.

As time went on, the Second Sight act became even more amazing. The secret, of course, was that he had devised a code so that he could inform Émile what the object was that he must name. This code was contained in the words and in the way these words were spoken when Houdin asked Émile to name the object.

The longer they worked together, the more code words Émile learned and the more he was able to tell about the object in question.

During the hottest part of the summer, the Paris theaters closed. Houdin then gave private Second Sight performances in homes of the nobility.

As they were preparing for several of these, Houdin received a royal command to present his magic and Second Sight to the court of Louis Philippe, the Citizen King of France.

The entire Houdin family was excited. There was no higher honor for a performer than to receive an invitation for a command performance before the royal family.

He immediately canceled all his engagements and went to work preparing for the show he would give for the king. He scoured Paris until he found several identical rusty iron boxes. Then he sent Mme. Houdin to a famous store that supplied the king's household. She was to buy a quantity of handkerchiefs of the exact type sold to the royal family.

Louis Philippe did not look his seventy-three years. He still had in him much of the soldier who had forsaken royalty to fight for the common people in the French Revolution.

Also present at the show were Queen Marie, and—most interested of all—the king's sister, the Duchess of Orléans.

The royal party received the magician in the drawing room of the palace in Saint-Cloud. Houdin and his son entered and bowed very low before the king.

"Welcome, Monsieur Houdin," the king said. "It was most gracious of you to come. However, we must warn you that we intend to make things as difficult as possible for you!"

"I welcome the challenge, your Majesty," Houdin replied.

Houdin did not bother with the usual magic tricks. Magicians had appeared in the royal court before, and all the common tricks would be familiar to the royal family. Houdin wanted to make his appearance completely different from anything they had seen before.

He and Émile opened with a demonstration of Second Sight. The members of the royal family vied with each other to produce curious objects that they hoped would stump Émile.

Finally the Duchess of Orléans suddenly left the room. She returned with a brocade box.

"Monsieur Houdin!" she said, her eyes sparkling.

"Your Grace," Houdin said with a courtly bow.

"I am positive that in some way you are informing your son of what you see. I have listened very carefully to your words, hoping to detect your code. Unfortunately for me, it is too clever. I have not been able to find out what it is."

"Perhaps that is because there is no code at all," Houdin said with a smile.

"There must be. So I have prepared a little trap for you. I wish your son to tell me what is in this box, but I forbid you to open it until after he has told us what is inside."

Houdin tried to look uneasy, although he was smiling inside. He was well prepared for such a trick. He thoughtfully fingered a large, curiously carved ring he wore on his left hand. Then he said,

"I would be most delighted, but Émile's Second Sight must see through the thick bandages on his face. It is asking too much for him to see through this box as well."

"Then he cannot see with his Second Sight unless you see the object and secretly let him know what it is," the duchess cried in triumph. "Admit it, Monsieur Houdin! I have exposed your trick!"

"Your Grace is very clever," Houdin said. "I am sure that it *might* be possible to fake Second Sight in the way you mention."

"Might? You mean that you do not do the trick in this manner?" the king asked.

"It is not necessary for me to see what is in this box for Émile to tell us what it is," Houdin said positively.

"But because it is such a strain on the boy, you do not wish to do it," the duchess said with a smile. "Very well, Monsieur Houdin. We will let you get away with this excuse. You have given us a very good show. I just wanted you to know that you cannot fool me!"

"I beg permission to continue," Houdin said. "I think that perhaps Émile can tell us what is in this unopened box. It is a great strain, that is true. But if his Majesty will give me permission to make this our last Second Sight trick tonight, it will give Émile time to rest afterward and no harm will be done to him."

"But you are not going to stop so soon," Queen Marie said. "You promised us a two-hour show."

"I have a new trick which I have just invented. With his Majesty's permission, I will show it after Émile does this last Second Sight for her Grace."

"Pray do so, Monsieur Houdin," the king said. "We are as interested as her Grace in seeing your son tell us what is in a box which we know you have never seen before."

"He will do so, your Majesty," Houdin said with a low bow.

"Her Grace has suggested that I am telling my son what to say by using a secret code in the words I speak. This time I will not speak to him at all. Will you give the commands to him, your Grace?"

"I will be delighted," the duchess said.

"Very well," Houdin said. "Let me hold the box here in a line with the boy. Please watch me and watch him, too. He might be up to some trick also!"

As he said this, all the party glanced at blindfolded Émile. It was only a second their eyes were away from Houdin. But this was long enough. His practiced fingers gently cracked open the brocade box. He could not risk raising it up to look inside, but this was not necessary. With his thumbnail, he flicked open the top of the special ring he wore. There was a tiny mirror inside. It reflected a glimpse of the inside of the duchess's box. Instantly Houdin snapped it shut and closed the mirror ring, which he had used many times in the theater for just such tricks as this.

"Are you ready, Émile, my son?" he asked and cleared his throat.

"Yes, Father," the boy replied.

"Then kindly listen to her Grace and answer her questions

as you would answer my own. I pray you to work hard with this most difficult trick. Please do not disappoint his Majesty, who has been so kind to us tonight."

In this speech were hidden a half dozen answers Émile needed to know. When he used the words "my son," he told the boy that it was jewelry. The clearing of his throat told him that there were diamonds, and the word "difficult" revealed that the article was a pin. And so on until every secret was passed to the boy.

Then Houdin bowed to the duchess. "Please, your Grace, you are now the magician."

The duchess leaned forward, her eyes sparkling. "Tell me, Émile," she said, "what is in my box?"

"It is very hard to see," the boy said in a faint voice.

He had worked on stage with his father long enough to know how to drag out a scene for dramatic effect.

"Then you cannot tell me?" she asked.

"I will try, but it is so very hard."

"If it is too hard and tires you too much, please say so."

"I would like to try. My father has never let me do this before. I would like to know if I can do it myself."

Houdin felt a glow of pride in his son. He had not instructed the boy in what to say. All this was Émile's own idea and he was doing splendidly.

"I see—something—it glitters—like jewelry," Émile said faintly.

The king smiled. "A very clever guess."

"I think there are nine diamonds—in a circle—please, may I rest just a moment?"

The king leaned forward, the smile fading from his face, when Émile mentioned nine diamonds in a circle. He looked surprised and very interested.

He looked across at the startled duchess. "The . . . uh . . . thing in the box," the king said. "Is it the . . . present . . . we gave you last Christmas?"

The duchess nodded her head. She looked thoughtfully at Émile. "Are you rested now?" she asked.

"Yes, your Grace," he replied politely.

"Can you describe the article in the box better than just by saying it is a circle of nine diamonds?"

"Yes, your Grace. It is a pin. At the top is a circle of nine diamonds going around a large red ruby."

"This—this is amazing!" the duchess cried.

"Yes!" said the king. "I would not have believed it possible had I not heard and seen it myself!"

"That is all, Émile," Houdin said kindly and proudly. "You have done well."

"Wait!" The Duchess of Orléans got to her feet. Houdin felt a flash of anxiety, wondering what difficult test she would put them to now.

"Let me have the box, Monsieur Houdin!"

When he gave it to her, she went over and placed it in Émile's hands. "Take it, you dear boy!" she said. "It is my present to you for your wonderful Second Sight!"

8. The Great Houdin

For his new trick—performed in public for the first time—Houdin borrowed several handkerchiefs from the royal party. He selected three and made them into a little package.

"These handkerchiefs, after a wave of my magic wand, will be instantly and invisibly transported to any place in the world which you wish to name. I suggest only that it be some place close enough that you can personally check it yourself. Will you please write on these cards the place where you wish the handkerchiefs to be found."

He passed out the cards. There were a few left over. These he kept in his hand. When several members of the party had written down their choices, Houdin collected the cards and gave them to the king, who had not written one.

"Lest it be said that I did some trick with the cards, I beg your Majesty to select one. And whatever that card says will be my command."

Louis Philippe riffled through the cards. "This one desires the handkerchiefs to be found on the mantelpiece. That is too easy. This one says in the dome of the Invalides." That is too far away for us to check on you. Now here is a good one. It asks that the handkerchiefs be magically transported to the box that surrounds the orange tree at the end of the avenue.

"Very well, Monsieur Houdin. Those are your orders, but

first . . . let me dispatch two of my servants to make sure that no secret assistant of yours rushes these handkerchiefs over for you."

Houdin smiled and bowed to the king. "As your Majesty wishes."

He waited until the servants had gone. Then he put the three handkerchiefs under a cover. It was a large bell made of black glass. Houdin waved his wand and commanded his invisible messengers to carry the package away. When he raised the bell, the package was gone. A little white turtledove was in its place.

Houdin bowed to the king. "Now, sire, if your Majesty will send someone to ask your watchful servants to open the box at the orange tree and bring back whatever it is they find there . . ."

Louis Philippe gave the order. The box to which Houdin had referred was a four-sided container built around the trees to protect them.

In about a quarter hour the servants returned with a rusty iron box which looked as if it had not been opened in centuries. It was placed in front of the king. Louis Philippe looked sourly at it.

"Our handkerchiefs are supposed to be in *this* thing?" he asked.

"Sire, they are there and have been there for sixty years!"

"Impossible!" the king snapped.

He had the servants force open the box. Inside, covered with what appeared to be the dust of years, was a sealed letter. The king inspected the seal and gasped with astonishment.

"Why, it is the seal of Count Cagliostro, who has been dead for fifty-five years."

The king opened the letter and read: "This package was placed here by me this Sixth of June, 1786, among the roots of an orange tree to help in a magic act to be performed exactly sixty years to this day before Louis Philippe of Orléans and his family."

The king looked at Houdin with uneasy amazement. "This smells of witchcraft," he said. "This seal is genuine. I am very familiar with the works of the famous Cagliostro."

"And if your Majesty will open the other package," Houdin suggested.

Louis Philippe did and the royal handkerchiefs fell out.

"Now this is amazing!" the king said. "Truly amazing, Monsieur Houdin."

There was no prouder moment in the magician's life. He bowed, unable to speak.

"But *how* did you do it?" the duchess asked, her face reflecting her own astonishment.

Houdin smiled at her. "There can be only two possible explanations, your Grace," he said. "One is that I am a *real* magician and actually sent your handkerchiefs sixty years into the past for Count Cagliostro to hide for me. Or—I played a clever trick on you. It is for you to decide which!"

"I am almost ready to believe that you are a real magician!" the king said with a smile.

"And I, too," the duchess added.

After his acceptance by the royal family, Houdin's fame swept through France. His shows were jammed with people every night.

Then suddenly everything came to an end. The peasants and lower classes of France had become dissatisfied with Louis Philippe, whom they accused of playing up to the moneyed class. In the February Revolution of 1848 the king was forced to abdicate, and the Second Republic was established, with Louis Napoleon as President. There was some bitter fighting in Paris, and officials closed all theaters.

Houdin was too old and Émile too young for the army. So while the struggle went on, Houdin took his family to England, where he had a triumphant tour. He appeared before Queen Victoria, who praised his acts as highly as Louis Philippe had done.

In England, Houdin noticed the first signs that it was time for him to retire. Through his mistaken belief that the public would not accept a young magician, he had started very late in life.

His hands were getting a little stiff, and he found himself making mistakes. In London he was doing the old trick of borrowing a watch from a man in the audience. This was put into a bag and beaten to pieces—apparently—with a hammer. The broken watch was displayed, and then placed back in the bag where it was miraculously restored to perfect order.

But in making the switch, he dropped the real watch and broke it. It was almost as if the years had rolled back and he was again the scared young apprentice worrying about a burned hat. Now, of course, he could easily afford to pay for the broken watch. But he feared for his reputation if the story got out.

He hastily whispered for Émile to keep the audience entertained. Then he slipped backstage and reverted to his old profession of watchmaker to fix the watch himself.

He ran into trouble again when he was doing the Inexhaustible Bottle trick in Manchester, England. It was not his fault, but the experience was very painful to him.

The bottle trick began easily enough. Houdin took a large glass bottle. He showed the audience that it was empty. Then he poured some plain water into it, which he ostentatiously sloshed around and then poured out.

He waved his wand a few times while Émile brought him a tray of glasses. He asked the audience to name their favorite drinks. As they did he poured that drink from the bottle. Five different drinks came from the bottle. He proved they were real by giving the glasses to men in the audience.

In their enthusiasm to get a glass, the audience kept crowding closer and closer until they overran the stage. Houdin was knocked down and badly bruised. Worse yet, from his standpoint, was that his bottle was cracked, and he had no way to repair it. He worked on it half the night, but still it leaked.

The trick was done by having a bottle with five separate chambers built around a center compartment. Each tapered down to a very small neck hidden in the neck of the main bottle. These openings into the various compartments were so small that air could not enter when the bottle was tipped up. Air, of course, was necessary to make the liquid flow out, and it was provided by very small air holes that were drilled into the outside of the bottle—one air hole for each of the five compartments.

As long as Houdin's hand covered all five holes, nothing could flow from the bottle. It appeared to be empty when turned upside down. Then, if he wished wine to pour from the bottle, he had only to shift his hand so that the air hole into the wine compartment was open. Then, by re-covering that hole and uncovering another, he could make a variety of liquids, such as milk, coffee, or whatever he chose, all pour from a single (so it looked to the audience) bottle.

But with the bottle cracked, air could get into all the sections. He could no longer control the different liquids, and just got an undrinkable mixture. He had to discard the act.

During this English tour Houdin introduced one of his most famous tricks, which he had perfected just before making the trip. This was called Suspension Ethereene, or Ether Suspension. Ether had just been introduced into medicine and was still a mysterious thing to the general public. In the act Houdin passed a bottle of ether under his son's nose. Émile went to sleep. The boy was laid stiffly across two chairs. Houdin then propped a slender stick under the boy's arm and removed the chair supports. Émile was floating in plain view, supported only by the stick under his elbow.

Houdin himself never revealed the secret of the Floating

Body trick, but Harry Houdini claimed that Émile's body was fitted with a steel corset worn under his clothing and that the stick which appeared to be wood was really a steel bar painted to look like wood. While the boy's body was supported by the chairs, Houdin diverted the audience's attention and quickly fastened the upright steel bar into a socket in the corset worn by Émile. The act was a sensation.

The English trip was a huge success, and Houdin returned to France with a lot of money, much of which he immediately lost on an ill-advised trip to Belgium.

The Belgian trip was one long series of troubles. At the start the coach lost a wheel. Then, at the border, the Belgian customs official demanded that Houdin pay a 25 percent duty on the value of his equipment before he would be permitted to bring the show into the country.

"This is impossible," Houdin said. "I don't have that much money with me. I came here to make money, not to spend it. Besides, if I have to pay so large a tax, I will make no profit at all from this trip."

"I am only the collector," the official said. "I do not make the law."

"But the law places a duty on merchandise for sale. I am not going to sell this stuff."

"But you are going to sell a *look* at it," the Belgian said shrewdly. "To me that makes it come under the law."

"Well, to me it does not!" Houdin cried.

"And I don't care what it is to you," the equally hot-tempered customs man retorted. "We go here by what I say."

"I won't pay it!" Houdin cried.

"Then stay in France. We have enough penny-pinching misers in Belgium now without importing any French ones!"

Houdin stomped out in a rage. He went out to the coach, where Émile and Mme. Houdin waited for him.

"Shall I turn around and head back to Paris, sir?" their coachman asked.

"I wish I could," Houdin said grumpily. "But I have signed contracts to appear in Brussels. If I do not appear, I will have to pay large damages to the theater owners."

"Then you will pay this outrageous tax?" his wife asked.

"Not one cent will I pay that robber!" Houdin cried.

"What are you going to do? Wave your magic wand and make him go away?" she asked.

"I'll think of something!"

"Father, it is so cramped in the coach," Émile said. "Can I get down until we go on?"

"Yes, yes, son," Houdin said absently. "Now what can I do to turn the tables on this customs pirate?"

Through the window of the customs house Houdin could see the official sit down to a pot of tea that had been brought him. When he finished, there was one lump of sugar left. The man carefully wrapped this in his handkerchief and put it in his pocket.

"Look!" Houdin said grumpily to his wife. "That rascal calls me a miser and he saves even a tiny lump of sugar. He—"

He stopped, an idea forming in his mind as the customs man took out an old gold watch and looked at it.

"Émile!" Houdin said.

"Are we ready to go, Father?"

"We are ready to go into our act!"

"Here in the road?"

"A real magician can do magic anywhere," Houdin said. "Yes, even if our stage is a rutty road. Kindly go across the street and play with those stones along the wall. When I speak to you, I wish you to answer me, but do not look toward me. Pretend you are more interested in your play. Do you understand?"

"Yes, Father."

"We may not get into Belgium free, but I intend to scare one customs official right out of his boots. The law does not require a tax on our magic equipment. This rascal is trying to make me pay so he can put the money in his own pocket."

"What are you going to do?" Mme. Houdin asked.

"Do? What do I always do when trouble blocks our way, madame? I merely make a determined wave of my magician's wand. And—*poof! Hocus-pocus! Abracadabra!* The trouble vanishes! Tee-dee-dum-dum—dee-dee!"

He went off humming a tuneless little song to himself. The customs official folded his hands over his big stomach and smiled as Houdin walked over to him.

"You are ready to pay?" he asked greedily.

"No, I have decided not to take in my equipment at all," Houdin said easily. "It is not necessary. Instead of doing magic I will do only our famous Second Sight, which is the most amazing, the most stupendous, the most unbelievable trick ever shown to the public. My son Émile does it with his mind."

The official's smile turned sour as he saw the money slipping away from him.

"You use no equipment at all in this Second . . . whatever it is?"

"None," Houdin said pleasantly. "It is all in the mind of my son—the lad you see playing across the road."

"Well . . . now . . . maybe I should tax *him*. After all, by your own admission, he is your equipment. Yes! I do believe that is what the law says."

"Monsieur," Houdin said, his smile turning frosty. "Do you know what Second Sight is?"

"I am too busy to waste time on magicians' humbug," the man retorted. "I know nothing of second or even third sight."

"Well, those gifted with Second Sight can read the mind of any man. There are no secrets safe from them."

"Impossible!" said the customs man.

"Oh, is it so? Very well, kindly walk to the window, where you can observe my son. See that there is no one near him.

You know he has not been near you. Nor have you and I exchanged any words except about our business. Is this not true?"

"It is true," the official said.

"Very well. Émile! Please stop playing a moment. What does this gentleman have in his coat pocket?"

"A small lump of sugar wrapped in a handkerchief," Émile said without looking up from his play.

"Oh, but that is impossible. No one carries a lump of sugar in his pocket," Houdin exclaimed. He pretended to look embarrassed and said to the customs man, "A thousand pardons, monsieur. The boy has made a mistake. Please bear with me. I will try again."

He was closely watching the other man's face. The official was staring out the window at Émile. His fat face mirrored his surprise.

Houdin's hand slipped gently to the gold watch chain stretched across the man's broad stomach. Easily, with the practice of years, he pulled the watch out of its pocket, opened the case, instantly closed it, and slipped the timepiece back in its place.

"Now, Émile, my *dear* son. Please get this one right, or this gentleman will not believe you can *really* read minds and that no secret of his is *safe* from you. Does he have a watch?"

"Yes, sir," Émile replied, still not looking toward them.

"Describe it."

"The case has a large letter *P* carved in it. It is the same initial that is embroidered on the handkerchief which the gentleman's hand is touching."

The startled man jerked his hand from his coat pocket. He looked suspiciously at Houdin and then back at the boy.

"What time does the man's watch say it is?"

"Two minutes past two, but it is slow. The clock on the office wall is correct. It reads four minutes past two."

The official's face turned pale. He jerked out his watch

and swallowed hard when he saw that the boy was correct.

"Who is the maker of the watch?" Houdin asked.

"Norient and Company of Paris," Émile replied.

"Impossible!" Houdin said, again looking embarrassed. "I again beg your pardon, monsieur. Norient are the most expensive watchmakers in France. It is obvious that a poorly paid customs officer could never afford such a watch as a Norient. The boy has made a mistake again."

"Yes, yes, a mistake," the man mumbled.

"Now, Émile, try to read the man's mind and tell how much money he made this month."

"I have no time to waste on such humbug," the man said quickly. "I have work to do. Kindly excuse me."

"Bon jour, m'sieur," Houdin said, bowing.

He called Émile and they got in the coach together. To the coachman he said, "On to Brussels, Pierre!"

They drove across the border as the customs officer watched, but he made no attempt to stop them.

Although his shows drew large crowds, Houdin actually lost money on the Belgian trip. He returned to Paris. The Second Republic under Louis Napoleon as President had restored order in Paris, and Houdin reopened his own theater.

Since none of his sons wished to follow in his work, Houdin started training his brother-in-law to take over the theater. This took two years. After that time Houdin started to do fewer and fewer shows. Finally he retired to a new home he had built at Saint Gervais, near his boyhood home.

He had long been interested in galvanism, or electricity. Just a few years before, in 1844, the American inventor and artist Samuel F. B. Morse had demonstrated the telegraph, and attempts were being made by scientists in England and America to make an electric light.

Except for an occasional performance in Paris to keep his hand in magic, he spent all his time working with electricity.

His home was an electrical marvel. He built a gadget that caused a table to rise out of the floor when he pressed a button. He used the telegraph principle to put a signaling device in his theater to make Second Sight easier.

His house was located one and a half miles from Blois beside the Loire River. The gate was quite a distance from the house, so he invented an electrical gadget to make it more convenient to use. As the visitor approached the gate, he saw a brass plate engraved with the words "Robert-Houdin." Below the nameplate was a gilt knocker and a sign inviting the visitor to use it. This knocker caused a bell to ring in the gateman's house a half mile away. The gateman then pressed a button which caused the gate lock to open.

Unfortunately, the gadget attracted too much attention. One afternoon the buzzer kept ringing in the gateman's shack. Each time he pressed the lock-opening button. Nothing happened. The buzzer kept ringing.

He thought something was wrong. He ran the half mile to the gate. There was no one there. He checked the electric circuit. It was in perfect order.

This went on for several days. Finally the gateman noticed that the ringing always happened at the same hour. The next day he hid at the gate. He found that a farmer, passing along each day, was amusing himself by watching the gate open automatically when he used the knocker.

"I just wanted to see how it works," he said when the angry gateman came up.

A few days later the gateman was returning from a visit in Blois. It was two o'clock in the morning when he passed the farmer's house. "This is where I get even," he told himself.

He beat heavily on the door. The farmer was not home, but his grown son came running in alarm.

"I just wanted to see how the door works," the gateman said sarcastically.

The young man, not knowing that the gateman was getting even with his father, punched him in the nose.

The next morning Houdin had to go to Blois and get his employee out of jail. He came home very dispirited.

"Trouble comes of everything I do," Houdin told his wife.

"The main trouble is that you miss your work," she said. "You do not like being retired. Why not go back to the theater?"

"I wanted to be the greatest magician in the world," he said. "I got my dream and I want very much to keep it. My hands are not as steady as they once were. I must quit while I am still called great. I do not want my audience to say, 'Ah, but he was great once.' Let them remember me as the Great Robert-Houdin."

"Oh, you are just talking yourself into trouble!" she cried. "For years you would not do the magic you love because you said you were too young. You were wrong, weren't you?"

"Yes, I was wrong," he admitted.

"And now you are doing the same thing by claiming you are too old. You are just as wrong!"

He smiled at her. "I wish you were right," he said.

"But I am right! You wait and see. You have invented Second Sight, Monsieur Robert-Houdin, but I, Madame Robert-Houdin, am the inventor of Third Sight! With this I can see tomorrow! And do you know what I see?"

"No, madame, I do not know."

"I see M. Robert-Houdin doing things so wonderful they will make all he has done before seem like child's play. So there! You just wait and see."

She was only making a joke to cheer him out of his sad mood. But, to the surprise of both of them, she proved to be right.

9. Duel in the Desert

The next day two visitors came to Saint Gervais to see Houdin. One was a tall, soldierly man. The other was short and wore a Vandyke beard.

"Permit me to introduce myself," the bearded one said. "I am Pierre Caron of the French Foreign Office. With me is Colonel de Neveu of our Foreign Legion army in Algeria."

Houdin expressed his pleasure at their visit, but it puzzled him. He started to worry that perhaps something he had done during his trips abroad had caused trouble for France. He could think of no other reason for the Foreign Office to be interested in him.

"Since Colonel de Neveu is the author of this odd scheme," M. Caron said, "I will permit him to outline it for you."

"Ah, yes," the colonel said. "Some years ago, a rebel Arab chief named Abd-del-Kadar led a revolt against France. He was defeated, but only after many Algerians and many Frenchmen were killed.

"Now we are afraid there is going to be another revolt," the colonel went on. "Some priests called marabouts claim to have supernatural power. They are doing magic tricks to convince the superstitious natives of this. If we do not break the power of these marabouts, they will soon cause another war."

"It seems to me that all you have to do is throw these marabouts in jail."

"That would make martyrs of them. What I want to do is prove their so-called supernatural powers are only tricks," the colonel said.

"Yes, Monsieur Houdin," the foreign office official said. "The colonel's idea is to expose these fakers by sending over a French marabout—you! I have seen your shows and you are a greater magician than these fakers."

Houdin was so amazed he could not speak. The colonel smiled and said, "What we are really asking, Monsieur Houdin, is for you to wave your magic wand and make a war disappear!"

"Just wave a wand!" Houdin said. "Monsieur, you sound just like my wife! Just wave a wand! You must all think I am a *real* magician."

"If you are successful, it will save many lives," de Neveu said.

"Then, gentlemen, what can I say except that I will try," the little magician said.

And true to his promise, Houdin went to Algeria to try and make a war disappear. He had expected some difficulties, but his first experience with the vindicative marabout in the marketplace and at his first performance indicated that he was in for serious trouble when he made his open-air appearance.

The night before the village performance, Jean Eugène Robert-Houdin stood at the window of his hotel in Algiers. The stars were brilliant over the ancient city and the domes and minarets were dark shadows against the sky.

He had been standing there for over two hours, thinking back over his eventful life. He knew that in a few hours he had to do a trick which, if anything went wrong, could bring his life to an end.

But this was a risk he took willingly. It made him proud to be able to do it. For a long time it had saddened him that he had never been able to do anything for the country he loved except amuse its people.

Now for the first time he had an opportunity to serve France like a soldier. If that meant death, it was a risk he would take without regret. But also like a soldier, although he was willing to die for his country, he preferred to serve it and live too, if he could.

When he had asked Mme. Houdin to get him the candle, spoon, and penknife, he had an idea how he could do the trick of catching a bullet in his teeth in plain daylight. But the chances of failure were so great that now he was not sure he should risk it. His initial flush of enthusiasm had faded, and he worried that his hands might no longer have the feather touch necessary to carry out the plan.

Finally he shrugged. There was no point in worrying until he tried it.

He walked over to the table where Mme. Houdin had left the articles for him. He cut the candle in two. One half he lighted and stuck up in the center of the table. The other half he shaved into little pieces. These shavings were separated into two piles. One pile was placed in a small dish and melted over the candle flame. This was set aside.

He took the knife blade and held it in the candle flame until it was covered with soot. Part of this was scraped into the wax from the melted candle. From time to time he compared the color with a real bullet. When the two exactly matched, he brought a bullet mold from his trunk. He poured three molds full of the lead-colored wax.

When it began to harden, he turned the mold over. Only a thin coat had hardened against the sides of the mold. The liquid inside ran out, leaving Houdin with a hollow wax bullet.

He opened the mold and found that he had turned it too quickly. The shell was too thin. It broke when he tried to pick it up. He remelted the wax and remade several fake bullets strong enough to handle, but thin enough so they would be destroyed when the gun fired.

By the time he was satisfied, Mme. Houdin was up. She saw what he was doing.

"You intend to palm the real bullet and put this wax shell into the gun," she said.

"Yes," he admitted. "In the sunlight the wax will look exactly like real lead."

"But it is so fragile," she said. "You have to move so fast to make the switch. I don't see how you can help breaking the wax shell with your fingers."

"I must be careful," he said.

"Even so," she said, "you are going to have trouble."

"If that happens—well, then we will stand revealed as fakers."

"But you remember what the colonel told us. The people in this village are fanatics. If they catch us trying to fool them—well, the colonel said they might shoot us."

"I am a magical soldier, remember. I must take risks. I don't want you to worry while we are gone. Everything will be all right."

"What do you mean . . . while you are gone! If you think for one minute that I will stay behind. . . !"

"Now, madame, a woman's place is in the home."

"My home is where you are, and that is my place!"

"Please, don't shout. You'll wake the whole hotel!"

He finally agreed to let her go. About noon the coaches came for them. They arrived at the village in the midafternoon. It was only a small cluster of mud shacks, but it was the center of some of the marabouts' strongest supporters.

A half dozen of the false prophets had gathered there. When the Europeans arrived they were already giving a demonstration of their magic. Houdin and de Neveu went over to watch. Since they were trying to impress the unruly natives with the power of the French, they had brought no soldiers with them.

Mme. Houdin remained in the coach to connect some batteries hidden under the seat with a wire running to an electromagnet in the baggage rack at the back of the coach.

When the two Frenchmen arrived, one of the marabouts was just drawing his sword. He placed the saber, blade upward, across two stands. Then two other marabouts helped him on top of it. He stood on the naked blade, holding to their shoulders for support.

The assembled natives cheered at this proof that their prophets were so tough even the blade of a sword could not harm them.

Ali, the marabout who had challenged Houdin in the theater, invited the French magician to stand on the sword.

"Tell the people," Houdin said to de Neveu, "that I have a better way of showing my power. I am not strong like their marabouts. But that is not important, for I have the power to take away their strength. After you tell them that, ask their strongest man to step forward."

When the Foreign Legionnaire had finished translating, a bull of a man stepped from the crowd. Huge muscles rippled under his sunburned skin. He looked like an Arabian Hercules.

"Are you very strong?" Houdin asked.

"I am the strongest man in the world," the Arab replied.

"Will you remain so?"

"As long as it is the will of Allah."

"You are wrong, for in just one minute I will take your strength away with my magic."

The Arab laughed. Houdin pretended to be angry.

"So you do not believe me? Very well. Do you see this box?"

Houdin walked over where a small box of metal sat on the baggage boot at the back of the coach. "Will you try to pick up this box?"

The Arab lightly lifted the box, which could have have weighed more than ten pounds. When he replaced it, Houdin asked if it was heavy.

"As heavy as a box of air filled with the lies of the French," the Arab said, and his companions whooped with laughter.

"Very well then," Houdin said, making a strange sign in the air with his hands. "Behold! You are now as weak as a woman. Lift the box!"

The muscle man sneered and reached for the box. He looked startled and tugged harder. Still the box refused to budge. He shot an uneasy look at Houdin. He stepped back, spat on his hands, and grabbed the box again. His muscles bulged. Cords stood out in his neck, and sweat started to streak his face.

Finally he stepped back, red-faced and worried.

"Perhaps you wish to try again," Houdin said. "It is really a very light box. See?"

He picked it up lightly and held it up for all to see. Then he replaced it. With a light wave of his hand, he again invited the Arab to try.

This time the man did not seem so confident. He threw his arms around the box and pulled with all his strength. When he was again unable to move the box the little Frenchman had handled with one hand, the frightened Arab was at last convinced that Houdin had indeed robbed him of his strength. He fell in the sand and raised his arms to heaven, imploring Allah to restore his lost power.

The marabout, worried at this display of power, reminded Houdin that he was supposed to catch a bullet in his teeth.

"As you wish," the Frenchman said. "Have you brought a gun?"

The Arab brought a muzzle-loading flintlock from under his burnoose. Houdin inspected it gravely. He handed it back with the words, "Please load and fire it. I wish everyone to know that it is a real gun."

He watched carefully while the marabout poured in powder from a horn and inserted the wadding and then the bullet, followed by more paper wadding.

When this was done, he fired the pistol into the ground.

After the gun had cooled and more powder been poured in, Houdin selected one of the lead slugs offered to him by the marabout. He inspected it carefully and held it up for all to see.

In the palm of the hand that held it was the wax bullet. It was hot here in the desert. The heat of Houdin's hand was causing the wax to soften.

It was going to be difficult—perhaps impossible—to make the switch smoothly between the real and the wax slug.

Houdin waited impatiently for the marabout to finish priming the gun. By the time he had, the wax bullet had stuck to Houdin's hand.

He could not go on. Yet he feared to stop. He had two other wax bullets in cardboard cups in his pocket. The cups were to keep them from being crushed. The problem was to find the right excuse to delay the loading until he could exchange unnoticed the now badly misshapen wax bullet.

Playing for time while he frantically sought an excuse, he turned slowly, holding the real bullet up. It was as if he were making sure everyone saw the bullet.

Then he turned and held the real lead over the muzzle of the gun. Before dropping it in, he hesitated. He looked up at the marabout.

"You know I can do this," he said. "You saw me in the theater."

"In a theater anything is possible," the false prophet said, with a sneer twisting his dark face. "Here we are under the watchful eye of Allah. No tricks will escape his eye—or *mine!*"

"In that case," Houdin said. "I want everyone here to be convinced that I really catch the bullet in my teeth and that no trick is involved. You have placed your mark on this bullet so you will know it is truly the one loaded in the gun. I would like Sheikh Ben-Allem to make his mark on the bullet. And also for Colonel de Neveu to do the same."

Without waiting for the marabout to reply, Houdin walked over and held out the bullet for the sheikh to mark.

While this was being done, Houdin quietly put his hand in his pocket. He took a deep breath and let it out, feeling better.

He did not take out another wax bullet. He knew it would only melt in his hand as the first had done. He waited until he received the real bullet back.

Taking it in his left hand, he held it up so everyone could see that he was not exchanging it for something else. He went over to the marabout, who raised the gun for Houdin to insert the bullet.

Houdin ignored the gun and shoved the bullet under the marabout's nose. "I want you to check the marks," he said. "Look at them closely."

While everyone's eyes were on the bullet, Houdin's right hand slipped into his pocket. When it came out, the wax-bullet shell was in the palm. He casually closed his hand over it and held up his thumb and index finger to which he transferred the lead slug.

"I am ready to load," he said quietly. "Have you checked the gun?"

The marabout momentarily looked at the pistol. "It is ready to kill you!" he shouted in Arabic.

The crowd howled with glee. And in the moment, when

their attention was diverted, Houdin switched the two bullets. Now it was the real lead hidden in the palm of his hand. The wax bullet was held aloft between his thumb and index finger.

He waited a moment. He was in an agony of suspense wondering if anyone had seen the quick, smooth exchange.

He wanted badly to shove the fake bullet into the barrel and get it out of sight as quickly as possible. He had to force himself to hold it steady above the gun. If he got panicky, it could arouse suspicion.

He remembered very well Colonel de Neveu's warning that if the tribesmen caught him tricking them, they might be so outraged that they would attack.

The wax was softening under his fingers. He could feel the sides giving in. He could wait no longer!

He pushed the wax bullet into the muzzle.

"Now!" he cried to the marabout. "Put in the wadding. I am ready to show these fine tribesmen that the magic of France is greater than the false lies you tell them!"

If the marabout had any suspicion that Houdin had switched bullets, it was lost in the flash of rage that swept him at the Frenchman's insulting words. He shoved the wadding into the gun barrel with a ramrod and turned the gun so it pointed at Houdin's heart.

"Killing you will be the greatest pleasure of my life!" he cried in French.

Houdin raised his handkerchief to his lips and coughed. At the same time he slipped the marked bullet into his mouth.

"Are you sure you wish to go throught with this, Monsieur Houdin?" Sheikh Ben-Allem asked suddenly. "And is it understood by the French authorities that you have asked for this and we will in no way be responsible for your murder?"

Houdin was appalled. He had the bullet just behind his

teeth so he could instantly force it out when the gun fired. He couldn't reply without revealing it. Nor could he switch it to his cheek without making suspicious movements.

On the other hand, he could not ignore the sheikh. For a moment he felt panic. It was terrible to work so hard and have everything fall to pieces just at the moment of success.

All he could do was bow to the Arab chieftain and hope that this would pass for an answer. Then, before anyone else could ask him an embarrassing question he could not answer, Houdin walked quickly over so that his back was to a mud hut. He waved to the marabout and waited for the shot that could start or prevent a war.

The prophet raised the gun. It trembled, and he took his other hand and steadied his wrist. To Houdin it seemed that the man was taking an eternity to aim.

With each second the magician's worry increased for fear something would happen before the trick could be finished. He doubted that his nerves would stand going through all this again.

"Aiiieee!" the marabout cried. "Allah! Allah! Death to the foreign dogs!"

He pulled the trigger. Sparks flew as the flint hit the steel and threw fire into the pan. The gun exploded. Houdin staggered and opened his mouth to show the bullet firmly caught between his teeth.

There was a shocked silence—then an uneasy, superstitious murmur as Houdin walked over to Sheikh Ben-Allem and handed him the bullet.

The sheikh eyed it silently and then said in a tight voice, "It is the bullet. It has my mark! You are truly a great marabout yourself, Monsieur Houdin."

The real marabout tried to break the spell that gripped the tribesmen.

"It's a trick! It's a trick!" he cried.

"Of course," Houdin said with a smile. "And now will you take my place by the wall and let me shoot at you. Then you can show your people that you are as great a magician as I."

He reached for the gun and started to pour powder into it. The marabout watched him for a moment. Then he gave a stricken cry and fled from the village.

"We have won, Monsieur Houdin!" the jubilant de Neveu whispered in Houdin's ear.

Houdin *had* won. The tribesmen were so awed that the revolt was broken before it started, and the marabouts lost their power.

When Mme. and M. Houdin got on the ship to return to France, the governor and Colonel de Neveu were at the dock to bid them good-bye.

"Monsieur Houdin," the governor said, "there are no words to thank you for the service you have rendered us."

"It is not for you to thank me," Houdin said with a happy smile. "I am the one who must thank you. You have done me a greater service than I have you.

"All my life I have wanted to do something for my country. You have given me that opportunity and I will always be grateful. Now I can feel I have helped France. Thank you, your Excellency. Thank you, Colonel de Neveu."

Afterword

On his return from Algeria, where he had prevented a war by a wave of his wand, Jean Eugène Robert-Houdin continued to give an occasional magic performance.

Before his death from pneumonia in 1871, he found time to write several books. The most famous was his *Confessions of a Conjurer*, the story of his life. He also wrote two books on how to be a magician and a book about the electrical wonders in his house at Saint Gervais.

The Confessions of a Conjurer, or, as it was called in America, *Houdin's Memoirs*, became the most famous book on magic ever written. For years it inspired young men to become magicians. The famous American magician and escape artist Harry Houdini, whose real name was Erich Weiss, was so thrilled by this book that he took Houdin's name and added an "i" to it to make his own stage name.

Although Houdini turned against Houdin later in life, he admitted this much: "From the moment I began to study the art, Robert-Houdin became my guide and hero. What Blackstone is to the struggling lawyer, Hardee's *Tactics* to the would-be Army officer, or Bismarck's life to the coming statesman, Robert-Houdin's books were to me."

Other famous magicians have said much the same thing,

and today he is often referred to as "the father of modern magic." His inventive genius took old tricks and gave them new polish and new wonder. He took magic out of the streets and gave it dignity.

The Secrets of Robert-Houdin Revealed

Can you do the same tricks that Robert-Houdin did? The answer is yes—if you are willing to put in the hours of practice necessary to do them smoothly. The tricks themselves are no longer secrets. Many of them were revealed by the magician himself in a book called *Secrets of Conjuring and Magic,* which he wrote more than a hundred years ago. At the end of this book Robert-Houdin promised to write another book giving still more secrets. Unfortunately, he died before he could keep this promise. However, other magicians have written books that tell how these other tricks were done.

Some of Houdin's magic is so simple that the tricks can be done anywhere by anyone willing to practice them. Others require complicated stage apparatus, which sometimes, like the Magic Orange Tree, is expensive to build.

It is a matter of principle with magicians never to reveal the secrets of their profession to their audiences. The reason is simple enough. A magician's job is to mystify. There is no mystery if the audience knows how the trick is done. However, magicians do reveal their secrets to other magicians and to beginners. We will assume that you have an interest in magic, or you would not have read this book. Perhaps you would like to be a professional magician; or you may only want to learn sufficient magic to amuse your friends at parties. In either case we are not violating the magician's code by revealing how Robert-Houdin did the tricks described in this book.

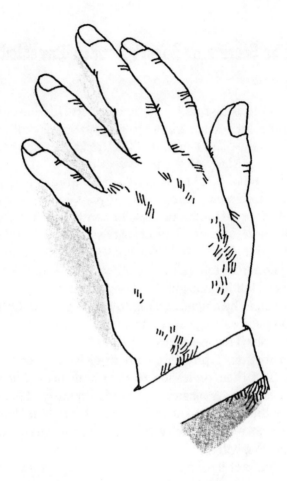

Fig. 1 Palming: What the audience sees.

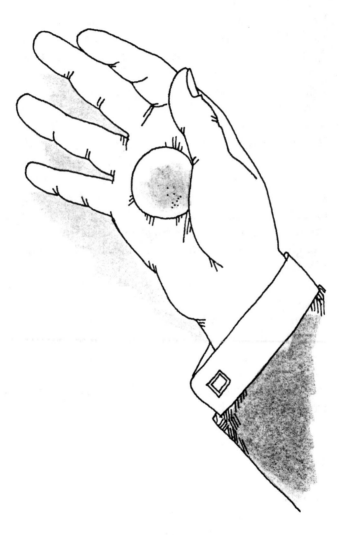

Fig. 2   Palming: What the magician sees.

Palming

The first tricks described in this book were those done by Robert-Houdin in the marketplace when he arrived in Algiers. Houdin made the marabout's watch vanish from the Arab's pocket and reappear in his own hand. Then he cut a peach and made it whole again; and finally he discovered a gold watch chain in a donkey's mouth.

All of these tricks depend upon one of the simplest and most basic tricks in a magician's repertoire. This is *palming*. Palming is the ability to hold small objects in the palm of one's hand in such a manner that the hand—seen from the back by the audience—appears to be open and is therefore assumed to be empty. (See Fig. 1.) The magician is helped in this deception because members of the audience understand that normally the fingers of the hand are not held straight as a board. They curve in, and this bending enables the magician to hold objects in his palm. (Fig 2.)

To pull the marabout's watch from thin air, Houdin first had to pick the Arab's pocket. This was done by diverting the victim's attention with a movement of one hand while the other hand lifted the watch. The watch was palmed until the magician was ready to make it appear. Houdin then reached quickly into the air and in a swift movement, too fast for the spectators to catch, his fingers grasped the watch from his palm, shoving it up into view so that it appeared to materialize from nowhere.

Finding the watch chain in the donkey's mouth was done in a similar manner. After the watch was secretly slipped from the marabout's pocket, Houdin first put the watch and chain into his own pocket. Here, while his left hand was performing a movement to attract attention, his nimble fingers unhooked the chain inside his coat pocket. Houdin's many years as a watchmaker aided him in this kind of trick. Then it was a simple matter to hold the chain in the palm of his hand—with the hand turned to conceal it from the spectators until he was ready to make it appear that he was taking the chain from the mouth of the donkey.

Restoring the Cut Peach

In his book on conjuring and magic, Robert-Houdin warned the beginner against slipping "vanishing articles" up the sleeve. He said it was too hard to keep the hidden articles up there. They had a way of slipping out at an embarrassing time. However, in this particular trick, working as he did in the open where he had no other receptacle to receive things, he went against his own advice. He tells us that when he selected a peach from the girl's basket, he used the cover of his hand to flip another one up his sleeve. He did not tell us the size of the peach, but we can assume that he was careful to pick small ones so they could be hidden during the palming.

After he cut the first peach in half, the magician restored it by holding the two halves up between his thumb and forefinger. (Fig. 3.) Just before placing the halves in this position, he had momentarily dropped his arm. This permitted the second fruit in his sleeve to drop unnoticed into his hand, where it was palmed while he placed the two halves of the first peach in position. Then he covered his hand with a large handkerchief. The whole peach was pushed up with his fingers while the split peach dropped into his sleeve. This was done very quickly, and it appeared to the spectators that the magician had no sooner draped the handkerchief over the split peach before he jerked the handkerchief off again to reveal the peach restored.

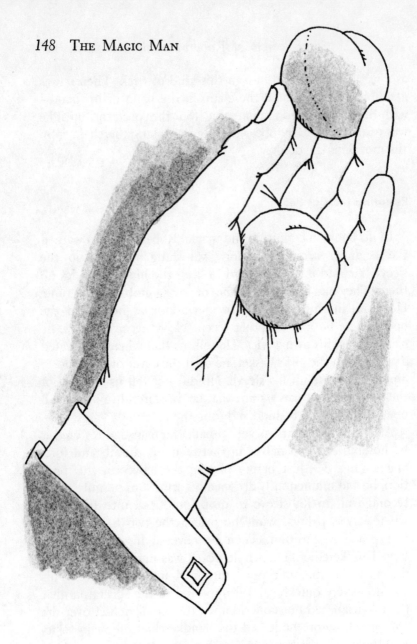

Fig. 3 Restoring the cut peach.

Had the magician been working on a stage, he would not have been forced to use his sleeve. He could have hidden the whole peach in any number of places around the stage and picked it up when he needed it.

The Threaded-Needles Trick

When M. Houdin apparently swallowed a spool of thread and a handful of needles and then drew the needles from his mouth all threaded on a single piece of thread, he again resorted to palming.

He first showed the loose needles and thread to the audience. Then, while he pretended to swallow them, the needles and thread were palmed, and while the audience's attention was diverted by a movement of his left hand, the palmed articles were dropped into his *servante*, a receptacle which the magician has unobtrusively placed behind his table or hidden behind other props on the stage.

In his mouth was a packet of needles that had been previously strung on a piece of thread, with knots between needles to prevent them from slipping. The needles were packed so that their *heads* pointed toward the magician's mouth. This precaution was necessary to prevent the sharp points from injuring his lips when he pulled them out of his mouth. The packet was placed in the magician's mouth earlier, in the side of his cheek, so it would not interfere with his patter and give away the secret that he had something in his mouth. (Fig. 4.)

Readers are cautioned against trying this trick themselves without expert supervision because of the sharpness of the needles. If not done correctly, there is danger of an amateur magician driving a needle into his tongue, lips, or jaw.

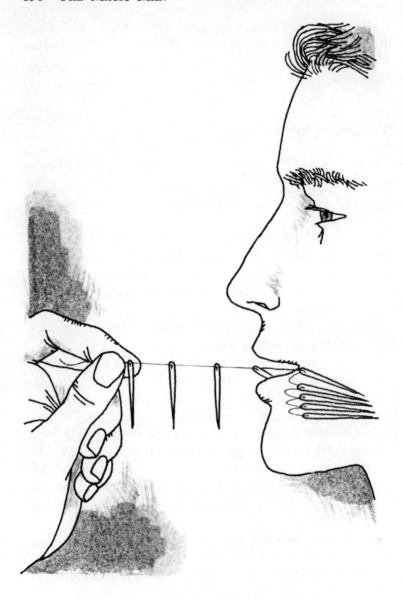

Fig. 4 The Threaded-Needles trick.

The Magic Goldfish Bowl

The production of a water-filled bowl with goldfish swimming in it is a surprising trick to see, but it is extremely simple in principle. Originated in China, it was a popular trick of European magicians. The magician on the stage shows his empty hands. Then he removes his flamboyant red-silk-lined cape and twirls it before the audience. A few seconds later the cape drops to the floor and the magician is seen holding a goldfish bowl so full of water that he can barely hold it; some of the water sloshes out. Several live goldfish can be seen swimming in the bowl to prove that it is indeed filled with water.

Here is the way it is done. A bowl is filled to the brim with water and then covered with a watertight cover. Originally this was oiled animal skin. This cover is so tight that the bowl can be hung either under the magician's coattails or behind his worktable without the water spilling. Then, as he twirls his cape with one hand, his other hand quickly takes the bowl from its hiding place, and with his thumb he loosens the cover at the same time. The twirling cape, which hides all this, is held by the magician's thumb and forefinger. The remaining fingers of that hand catch the loosened cover, which is hidden by the cape as it drops to the floor. The dazzled audience sees only the magician holding the full bowl with fish swimming in it.

The difficulty in getting the waterproof cover off quickly and smoothly limited magicians before Houdin to the use of small bowls. But Houdin's inventive mind soon thought up a quick-release gadget, and this enabled him to use much larger bowls. Here is the way Houdin explained it, according to the English version of *The Secrets of Conjuring and Magic or How to Become a Wizard*, by Robert-Houdin, as translated by Professor Hoffman in 1878.

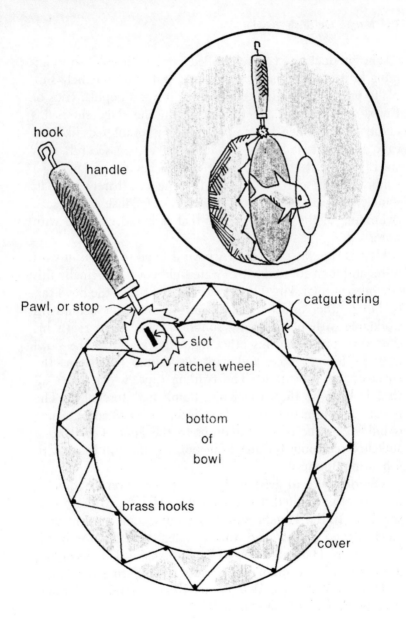

hook

handle

Pawl, or stop

catgut string

slot

ratchet wheel

bottom
of
bowl

brass hooks

cover

"Instead of the sheepskin cover, I took a piece of waterproof cloth, to which I fitted a certain mechanical arrangement in order to securely close the bowl.

"All around the edges of the cloth are attached little brass hooks. A piece of catgut, with a ring at each end, passes through all of these hooks and is attached to two points placed one on each side of a little brass cylinder. It will be readily understood that by turning this cylinder with a key, you wind up the cord and thereby draw the cover tightly over the bowl. A ratchet wheel forms part of the cylinder and turns with it. This serves to retain the tension on the catgut string at any given point."

There is a stop mechanism at the end of a hook that engages the ratchet and keeps it from unwinding. This hook also serves as a means of hanging the bowl where the magician chooses to hide it. The stop was so made that it locked the ratchet as long as the bowl hung in a downward position. Once the bowl was turned upright, the tension went out of the catgut string and the cover came off in the magician's hand. (Fig. 5.)

"Under these circumstances," Houdin wrote, "the execution of the trick is instantaneous."

Fig. 5   We are looking at the bowl from the *bottom*. The closely fitting waterproof *cover* is pulled tight by *catgut string*, which is attached to the cover by small *brass hooks*. The cover is tightened around the bowl by turning the *ratchet* wheel by means of a key inserted in the *slot*. A *pawl*, or *stop*, engages the ratchet teeth to keep the ratchet wheel from unwinding and loosening the catgut string. The *handle* serves to release the ratchet; *hook* on its end holds the bowl in its hidden place till needed.

Insert: Fishbowl in hanging position.

The Vanishing Person

On the stage in Algiers, Houdin made his wife vanish. At other times he performed the same trick with his son. The Vanishing Person trick is a favorite magician's act, and there are many ways of doing it. One way is to put an assistant in a closet that has a turntable back. When the closet door is closed, the assistant spins around and stands on a ledge in back of the new back wall when the magician opens the door. One magician employed an acrobat for an assistant. He vanished under cover of a screen by grabbing a trapeze and swinging out of sight.

Houdin, however, relied on black velvet and the soft candlelight that illuminated his stage. He performed this trick in front of a large backdrop of black velvet. The pile surface of black velvet does not create reflections. So when Robert-Houdin placed a smaller black velvet screen in front of the large black backdrop, the screen blended with the background and was invisible to the audience.

For the trick, Mrs. Houdin stood near one end of the smaller screen. When Houdin twirled his cape between her and the audience, all she had to do was to step quickly behind the screen. When the cape fell, she had vanished. To make her reappear, the magician had only to twirl the cape again to hide her swift movement from behind the screen. (Fig. 6.)

Fig. 6   The Vanishing Person. (*a*) Black velvet background. (*b*) Smaller black velvet backdrop. (*c*) Person about to vanish. (*d*) Magician. (*e*) Cape or other screen.

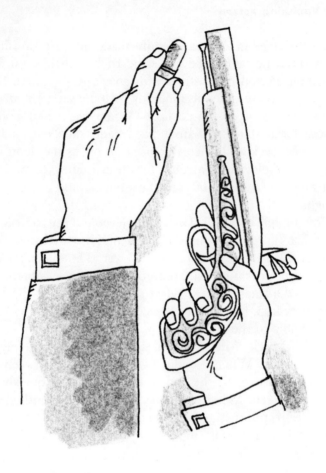

Fig. 7   The Magic Bullet: What the audience sees.

The Magic Bullet

In his autobiography Houdin claims he learned this trick from Torrini, who killed his own son while performing it. In any event, Houdin did the trick, and where he learned

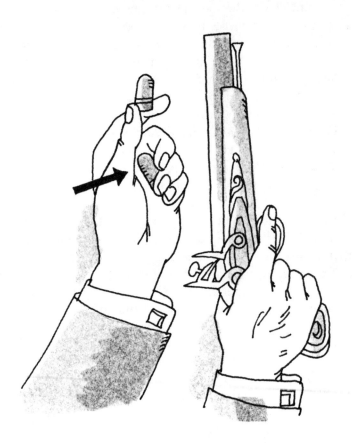

Fig. 8 The Magic Bullet: What the magician sees.

it is probably not important. Houdin performed the trick in this manner: He displayed a real lead slug and had a witness from the audience mark it for future identification. Then Houdin used sleight of hand to palm the real bullet and substitute a bogus one in its place. (Figs. 7 and 8.) The bogus bullet was dropped down the barrel of the gun—they still used muzzle loaders in those days—and then was jammed into place with a ramrod. On the stage Houdin used a gray paper bullet, which was torn to pieces by the explosion of the powder. As he took his place across the stage to make a target for the person chosen to shoot the gun, the magician secretly slipped the real slug into his mouth. When the gun fired, Houdin staggered as if hit. This heightened the suspense. Then, as he raised his head, he opened his lips and disclosed the bullet held between his teeth. On inspection, it proved to be the one the witness from the audience had marked.

Houdin could not use the paper bullet in the desert, for the bright sunlight would reveal the fake. Instead, he made a hollow bullet from gray wax.

In his own act, Torrini did not catch the bullet in his teeth, as Houdin did later. According to Houdin, his old teacher used his son as a target. The boy placed an apple on his head and Torrini fired at it in a modernized version of the William Tell legend. After the gun was fired, the apple on the boy's head was cut open and the bullet was found inside. The apple was specially prepared with a small hole cut in the side. This was covered by the magician's hand and the marked bullet slug pushed into the hole while the magician placed the apple on his son's head. Then, when the apple was cut open and the bullet revealed, the half with the hole was discarded before the audience got an opportunity to inspect it.

A Note of Caution: The Magic Bullet trick, involving the switching of a real cartridge for a fake one, is a dangerous act. It is one that an amateur magician should never attempt. It seems simple to switch the bullets, but in the excitement of performing the act, it is easy for the beginner to get confused and reverse the switch, with fatal results. This is what must have happened when Torrini accidentally killed his son with the trick.

In 1946 a French writer, to answer the American escape artist Houdini's earlier attack on the memory of his former idol, investigated the history of Robert-Houdin to find out how much truth there was in the old magician's memoirs. He verified the major part of it, but was unable to find any historical reference to Torrini. He concluded that Robert-Houdin invented Torrini to add drama to his story. However, there is another explanation, namely, that Robert-Houdin *did* know such a man, but that, because of Torrini's tragic past, he used a pseudonym instead of the magician's true name.

This is reasonable because the rest of Robert-Houdin's story stands up under critical inspection. It is a story dramatic enough in itself, and the author had no call to add one fictitious incident to it.

The Miraculous Fruit Tree

In this trick a seed is planted in a box, and while the box is hidden by a cover, a small fruit tree grows from it and bears flowers and fruit before the audience's eyes. Houdin did not reveal its secret, but Harry Houdini, in his book *Unmasking Robert-Houdin*, quotes from a book published in 1790:

"The branches of the tree may be made of tin or paper, so as to be hollow from one end to the other in order that air which enters at the bottom may find its way to the top of the branch. These branches are so adjusted . . . with leaves made of parchment that the whole ensemble closely resembles nature."

This mechanical mechanism, collapsed so that it takes up little room, is enclosed in a small flat box. Then "under cover of a cloth a confederate blows air through a glass tube which causes the tree to 'grow.' " (Fig. 9.)

Houdini goes on to tell us that originally the tree produced only leaves and flowers. Then "later it was described as being accomplished by springs and real fruit was stuck on the tree and the leaves were so secured around the fruit that at first appearance they could not be seen. Then a piston was used to spread the leaves and make the fruit appear."

Fig. 9 The Miraculous Fruit Tree. (*a*) Air hose. (*b*) Air hose inside tree trunk and branches. (*c*) Cover which hides "growing" tree.

The Shower of Flowers

Today this is generally accomplished with spring-loaded artificial flowers. The petals are pressed flat and thus take up little room. When released from the cone in which they were packed, the springs open the petals and the pile of flowers then appear to be several times what could have been packed in the cone.

Omelet in a Hat

In this trick the magician breaks a raw egg into a hat and then cooks it over a candle flame. Perspective is the secret of this ancient trick. The borrowed hat is placed on the magician's table in such a way that the side is visible to the audience, but not the top. The hat must be higher than the audience. Then the egg is broken. The yolk and white are dropped *behind* the hat and fall into a receptacle hidden from the audience's view. (Fig. 10.) The angle of view from the auditorium makes it appear that the egg went into the hat. Now it is only necessary for the magician to pick up the hat and hold it over the flame of a candle. He must be careful, however, that the candle flame does not scorch the hat. This was Houdin's mistake in his first performance.

After the egg has been "cooked," it must be produced from the hat. This is greatly simplified by using a rubber omelet. The prop can be squeezed into a ball inside the palm and secretly transferred into the hat while going through the motions of getting the egg out with a ladle.

Fig. 10   Omelet in a Hat.

Second Sight

This is the trick that made Houdin famous. A blindfolded assistant sits on the stage. The magician in the audience asks him to identify certain objects that members of the audience pick out. It is obviously impossible for the assistant to see what the magician and the spectator have selected. However, he answers correctly each time. The secret, of course, is that the magician tells his assistant what the object is. Originally Robert-Houdin did this with a voice code. Certain words meant certain things. This required his son, Émile, to learn many code words. Houdin tells us how he and the boy would go window-shopping to devise new codes for objects they saw which might be used in their act.

Regardless of the ingenuity of a trick, soon the secret becomes known. Then the magician must devise new ways of doing the same thing. When the public began to suspect that he was talking to his son in code, Houdin had to invent a new way of doing his act. He no longer spoke to Émile himself, but asked the person selected in the audience to ask the boy to name the object. In this switch, Houdin's code was hidden in the conversation he had with the audience. This was a very small and obvious switch, but it was simple enough to allay audience suspicion for a time.

Later Robert-Houdin dispensed with the cumbersome and hard-to-learn voice code entirely. Houdin did not reveal this secret, but Harry Houdini claimed that Houdin did it with hidden buttons that activated electrical signals to inform Émile.

The Vanishing Handkerchiefs

This is the trick Houdin used to astound the court of Louis Philippe. Three handkerchiefs borrowed from the spectators were made to vanish and then reappeared in an antique iron box found under an orange tree in the street. Houdin carried the secret of this trick with him to the grave. In none of his books did he reveal the secret.

Harry Houdini, in *Unmasking Robert-Houdin*, tells how he did a similar trick and he felt that Houdin must have done it in this way. Performing before a lodge group in New York City, Houdini also borrowed three handkerchiefs from the audience and made them vanish. They were found in a box under the top step of the Statue of Liberty.

According to Houdini: "I borrowed three handkerchiefs and tied them together for easy handling. I had three other handkerchiefs, similarly tied together, under my vest. I switched the two sets of handkerchiefs, so that those furnished by the spectators were under my vest and the bogus handkerchiefs were in my hand."

Houdini laid the bogus handkerchiefs on the magician's table and started to cover them with an opaque glass bell. He then had a *deliberate* accident and broke the glass. Leaving the handkerchiefs on the table in full view of the audience, he walked to the wings, where an assistant handed him a new glass. Under cover of the glass, during the exchange, the assistant deftly snatched the real handkerchiefs from under Houdini's vest. (Fig. 11.) The assistant then rushed off to hide the handkerchiefs in a predetermined place.

In the meantime, the magician went back and began his act again. This was all timed so the assistant could just make the ferry going to Bedloe's Island and the Statue of Liberty. Houdini then distributed cards for members of the audience to

Fig. 11   The Vanishing Handkerchiefs.

write down the name of a place they wanted the vanishing handkerchiefs to appear. When these were collected in a hat, Houdini used sleight of hand to add three cards of his own. The three had the same place written on them: "Send the handkerchiefs to the top step of the Statue of Liberty."

In reaching his hand into the hat to pull out a card, he pulled out these three. Then, to impress the spectators that he was being completely fair, he refused to choose one of the three himself, but asked a child to pick one. Naturally it said for him to make the handkerchiefs vanish and reappear under the top step of the Statue of Liberty.

Houdini then proceeded to place the black glass bell over the bogus handkerchiefs and made them vanish by regular sleight of hand. The audience, of course, thought these were the real handkerchiefs. Now Houdini invited the spectators to choose a committee to go with him to the Statue of Liberty in New York Harbor, where, to their amazement, they found the original handkerchiefs soldered in a tin box under the top step of the stairs, exactly where Houdini's secret confederate had hidden it.

"This is probably," Houdini wrote, "the method used by Robert-Houdin to deceive the French monarch."

The Inexhaustible Bottle

This is another very old trick. Houdin did not invent it, but he used it to great advantage in his stage productions. The magician pours water into an opaque bottle. He sloshes the water around and then holds it upside down until all the water has run out. This is enough to convince even the most skeptical audience that the bottle is empty.

Once the emptiness of the bottle has been established, the

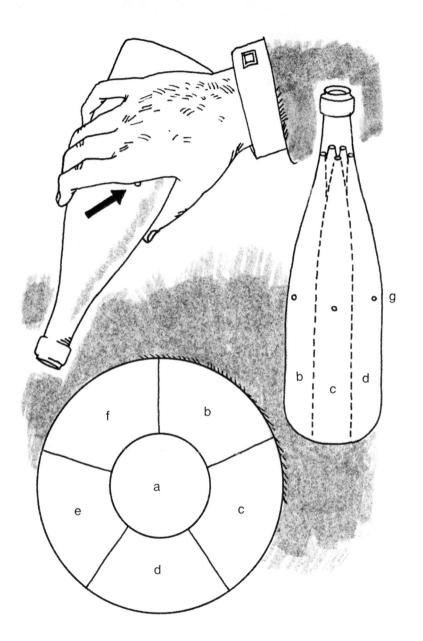

magician then proceeds to fill five glasses with five different-colored liquids poured from the supposedly *empty* bottle.

This is a very baffling trick. The audience has seen the bottle upturned and all the water poured out of it. Then, in addition to the mystery of how an empty bottle could possibly produce any more liquid, there comes the even more startling discovery that the apparently empty bottle contains not one, but five different liquids *without mixing them*.

It is done with air pressure. The bottle is divided into five separate compartments that surround the main bottle. Each of these compartments terminates in a very narrow neck hidden in the neck of the big bottle. The five compartments are filled with the desired drinks, which are usually selected for their contrasting colors. The center compartment has a larger opening so the magician can pour water into it and then dump the water to prove that the bottle is empty. The five liquids will not run out of their small necks because of air pressure. Air must enter the bottle in order for the liquids to flow out.

The secret is this: A small ring of holes is bored in the outside of the container, one for each of the secret compartments. When the magician first grasps the bottle, his hand covers all the holes. Nothing flows from the secret compartments. But he can obtain a flow from any of them simply by shifting his hand so that a particular hole is uncovered. By uncovering different holes in turn, the flow of the various drinks is controlled. This trick is sometimes done by science teachers as a demonstration of the effect of air pressure. (Fig. 12.)

The Floating Body Trick

Houdin never revealed the secret of this trick (Fig. 13), but Harry Houdini claimed that Émile's body was fitted with a steel corset worn under his clothing. The stick, which was painted to look like wood, was a strong steel bar. While the boy's body was supported by the chair, Houdin diverted the audience's attention and fastened the upright steel bar into a special socket in the steel corset worn by Émile. (Fig. 14.)

"Spectators and reviewers commented on the rigid, almost painful, carriage of Robert-Houdin's son during the performance," Houdini wrote. "Unquestionably Robert-Houdin used the crude corset-and-rod method of working the trick."

Houdini goes on to say, "This method was improved, first to make it a self-rising suspension, then eventually with a steel rod from the back of the stage, eliminating the need for rods under the arms."

The Floating Body

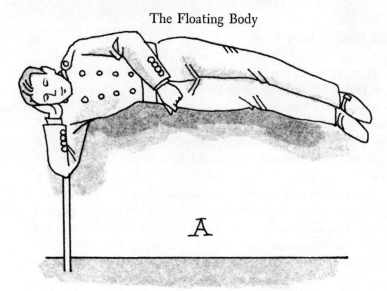

Fig. 13 What the audience sees.

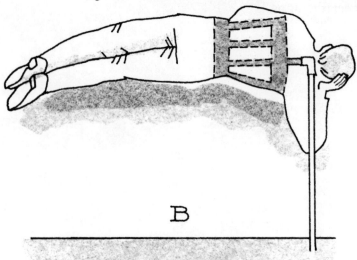

Fig. 14 What the magician sees.